metaLABprojects

The *metaLABprojects* series provides a platform for emerging currents of experimental scholarship, documenting key moments in the history of networked culture, and promoting critical thinking about the future of institutions of learning. The volumes' eclectic, improvisatory, idea-driven style advances the proposition that design is not merely ornamental, but a means of inquiry in its own right. Accessibly priced and provocatively designed, the series invites readers to take part in reimagining print-based scholarship for the digital age. www.metalab.harvard.edu

Series Editor
Jeffrey T. Schnapp

Advisory Board
Ian Bogost (Georgia Tech)
Giuliana Bruno (Harvard VES)
Jo Guldi (Brown)
Michael Hayes (Harvard GSD)
Bruno Latour (Sciences Po, Paris)
Bethany Noviskie (U of Virginia)
Andrew Piper (McGill)
Mark C. Taylor (Columbia)

Art Direction
Daniele Ledda
metaLAB and xycomm (Milan)

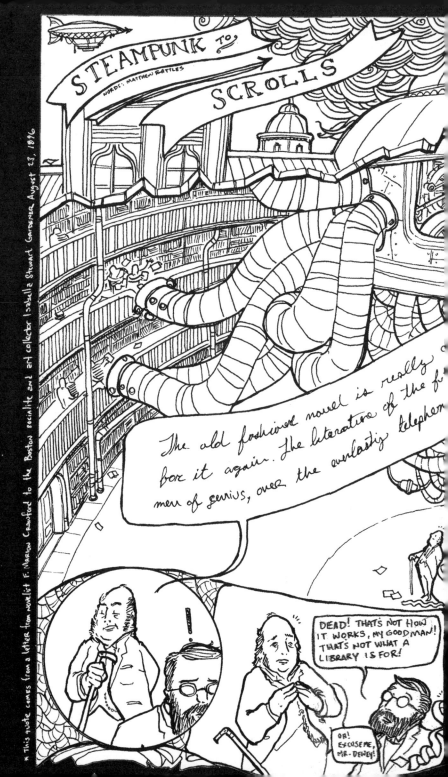

STEAMPUNK TO SCROLLS

WORDS: MATTHEW BATTLES

The old fashioned novel is really ⟨...⟩ for it again. The literature of the fu⟨...⟩ men of genius, over the everlasting telephon⟨e⟩

* This quote comes from a letter from novelist F. Marion Crawford to the Boston socialite and art collector Isabella Stewart Gardner August 23, 1896

!

DEAD! THAT'S NOT HOW IT WORKS, MY GOOD MAN! THAT'S NOT WHAT A LIBRARY IS FOR!

OH! EXCUSE ME, MR. DEWEY!

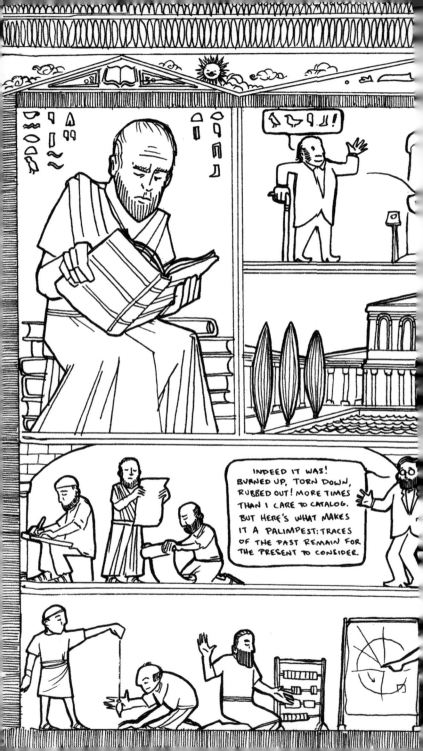

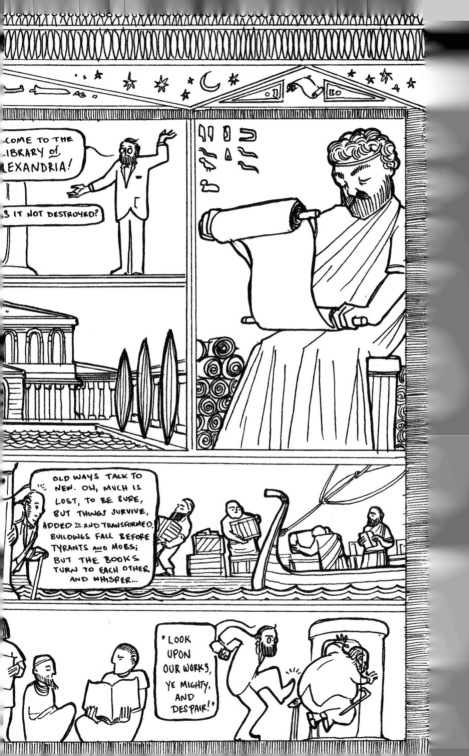

A MEDIEVAL SCRIPTORIUM

WE'RE IN THE GREAT LIBRARY OF ST. GALL, WHICH DATES FROM THE TIME of CHARLEMAGNE THE GREAT. MY GOOD MAN, THIS LIBRARY HAS SEEN ONE RENAISSANCE AFTER ANOTHER! INDEED IT HOLDS MANY MANUSCRIPTS — MORE THAN 2,000 — BUT NEARLY AS MANY PRINTED BOOKS, AS WELL.

AH, T

EVERLASTING, INDEED! BUT OLD JOHANNES NEVER DID SWEEP SCRIBBLING AWAY, NOT EVEN IN HIS BIBLE. THE PRETTY INITIALS, THE DECORATIONS, EVEN THE PAGE NUMBERS — ALL THE HANDIWORK OF SCRIBES! WHO WERE RUBRICATING, ILLUMINATING, AND GLOSSING PRINTED BOOKS FOR A GENERATION AFTER GUTENBERG GAVE UP THE GHOST.

THE OLD BO

INDEED! THE PRINTING PRESS BROUGHT A REVOLUTION, TO BE SURE. BUT IN DOING, IT REMIXED THE PAST. MORE LAYERS FOR THE PALIMPSEST!

SURELY, BU

CHANGE IS IN THE PALIMPSEST'S VERY NATURE! AFTER ALL, YOU STILL WRITE WITH A PEN, DO YOU NOT?

Wisdom builds her house,
but folly with her own hands tears it down.

Proverbs 14:1

Jeffrey T. Schnapp
Matthew Battles

‡‡‡‡‡‡‡‡‡‡‡‡‡‡‡‡‡‡‡‡‡‡‡‡‡‡‡‡‡‡‡

The Library
Beyond the Book

metaLABprojects

- - - - - - - - - -

Harvard University Press

Cambridge, Massachusetts, and London, England

2014

Library of Congress Cataloging-in-Publication Data

Schnapp, Jeffrey T. (Jeffrey Thompson), 1954-
   The library beyond the book / Jeffrey T. Schnapp, Matthew Battles.
      pages cm. — (MetaLABprojects)
   Includes bibliographical references.
   ISBN 978-0-674-72503-4 (alk. paper)
   1. Libraries—History. 2. Libraries and society. 3. Libraries—Aims and objectives.
4. Libraries and electronic publishing. 5. Libraries—Forecasting. I. Battles, Matthew. II. Title.
   Z721.S34 2014
   020.9--dc23

                        2013042383

Graphic Design:
xycomm (Milan)
Gennaro Cestrone
Stefano Cremisini
Francesca Farro

Table of Contents

< Provocations >
The Library Beyond the Book
some thought experiments

Prospects

The title of this volume is
a provocation, not a description.
It gestures toward a threshold being
traversed at the time of writing,
not toward an era when books
will vanish and bookshelves will be
seen only in virtual versions,
brimming over only with e-books.

The threshold in question is made
up of interlocking components:
changes in the nature and status of
the document and the book; changes
in practices of reading, research,
note-taking, and information sharing;

changes in the architectural and institutional containers in which such practices are carried out and by means of which they are supported. It was arrived at not suddenly but slowly, not with the wave of a digital magic wand, but thanks to a century-long transformation in the culture of communication.

Humanity has found itself on such thresholds before. Indeed, the modern predicament consists in precisely this posture on a brink, perpetually caught midway between taking flight and a fall. These thresholds seem to arrive in ever-shorter intervals, which halve themselves at each half-step like some kind of Hegelian riff on Moore's law, a logarithmic *accelerando* worthy of Zeno. Are we any closer to the—to the what? to the omega point, the apotheosis, the singularity? Now perhaps more than at any other time in the last half millennium, we tumble along this corridor of thresholds looking backward, angel-of-history-like, regarding the spectacle of shattered event-horizons tossed together in a historiographic *mise-en-abîme*. Once, the thresholds had piled up like a stairway to heaven. Now jumbled, they seem less a straight path than a hall of mirrors. We're midway on this journey beyond the book—and it's midway all the way down.

While the "beyond" in our title may trouble the wary reader, it's worth remembering that there were libraries *before* there were books—if by books we mean the consumer-product codex of the late twentieth century, which arrived not only in the form of a certain apparatus and set of material attributes, but as a regime of market forces, institutional arrangements, physical and technical structures, which interact with the material in historically contingent ways. The book as we know it is often casually termed "the invention of Gutenberg," although the goldsmith of fifteenth century Mainz would hardly know what to make of its barcode and ISBN; its digitally-prepared text and typography; its wood-pulp paper and covers of cloth and board or laminated paper stock; its precarious commodity network of printing plants, warehouses, and the market forces from preorder to remainder; the many forms it takes to suit social situations as varied as church sermons, travel, early childhood play, puzzle-solving, teaching, technical documentation; and the peculiar social and economic formations—bookstores, textbook depositories, mail-order reading clubs, to name a few—which it has been adapted to suit. These peritextual elements are anything but accoutrements. They combined to lend the book its most powerful qualities in the late age of print: ubiquity, fungibility, a finely-evolved balance of durability and disposability, the capacity to act as a consumer good that can be tracked from printing plant to bindery to shipping center to shop to resale network to pulping station.

A quarter century before the new millennium, most books were already electronic books: composed with word processors, designed in page-layout software, produced on computer-controlled presses, their embodiment in pulp and ink long has been a kind of artifactual reverse apotheosis, a mystification of the divide between container and contained. This congeries we call the book—the mass-market pulp, the trade hardcover, the paperback original, the coffee-table volume, the limited edition, the technical manual—is a remarkably flexible typology in material culture. Even now it has a rich and diverse future. But the conditions in which it takes up its peculiar qualities today have not always obtained. Nor will they obtain in the time to come. They will shift and change, raggedly and unevenly, in some dimensions more quickly and in novel directions. And, as has happened in the past, such change will manifest in the material, in the physical shapes through which knowledge makes itself immanent.

The domains of the material and social are never fully subordinate, one to another, but everywhere interdependent upon

Livebrary – libraries are beehives of activity, but much of that activity is invisible. The Livebrary is a touchscreen that allows users to experience the life of a library in real time: data flows; usage statistics; interlibrary flows; trending search patterns; books being taken out, returned, copied, and scanned. (JS)

and interactive with one another. As they change—as the book transforms—the material and institutional structures that express and reflect their peculiarities must transform as well. We see these changes taking place with respect to four qualities: Connection, Storage, Activation, and Architectonics (understood as the interplay between the container and the contained).

Through all of them runs the book beyond the book.

Connection

Much has been made of the discrete nature of the book: bounded, with beginning, middle, and end, cut off from the world within its covers. Hiding behind its title page, the words invisibly cradled within the structure of the folded and cut pages, the book can be said to be *discreet* as well. It's a medium that requires connections to be made in what the technofuturists call meatspace—among us in the world, ephemerally, reconfigurably. Silent reading, the normative practice of reading in the modern era, is a state of communion and secrecy; what passes between reader and reading-machine is only revealed through subsequent acts. (Of course, to interpret the cognitive work of reading as an offloading of connection and activation, whether figured as feature or bug, is to denominate a quality only visible in the context of computation.)[1] And since the time of Socrates—whose "books" were not the same as ours, much less Gutenberg's, because they were scrolls—the insularity, the single-mindedness, and the supposed fixity of written texts has troubled their critics. Over the long history of the book, we've developed a toolkit for overcoming this supposed fixity: library catalogs; bibliographies, indices, and concordances; syllabi and footnotes; learned journals for critical reflection and review; and various institutional and market structures. Instruments such as these have enabled us to elaborate connections from book to book, to turn text into a kind of hypertext. Affection for these affordances is understandable; the impulse to question the effects of their obsolescence is salubrious.

So when we write about "the library beyond the book," we don't mean the library *after* the book: merely that we intend to consider the case of the library beyond the constraints of bibliophilia and bookish nostalgia. After all, books have never been "just books." They were always coaxed to life by conversation and oration; the oral and written sharing of excerpts; practices of addition, deletion, and extension; swarms of mental or scribbled notes; acts of collation, from rebinding to anthologizing to the authoring of mimeo- or xerographic readers. They were also always surrounded by a halo of what we now call metadata of one kind or another: title or location tags, collections lists, cataloging data, records, descriptive captioning.

With the emergence of standard book-numbering codes (such as the International Standard Book Number, or ISBN, an elegant system for the cybernetic identification of books, adopted in 1970) and centralized cataloging systems like the MARC record embraced as the international standard in 1973 (as more than a mere data format but an entire techno-infrastructure), the halo has migrated from paper into the digital realm in the course of the past half century. Today, virtually no physical book is born without first being born as a data object—indeed, a flock of objects, a network unto itself—that circulates in advance of its appearance as a bound volume. With the advent of e-publishing, the halo has expanded to the point of displacing the very objects that it once supported. Nearly every book and every document now lives multichannel lives, raising a tangle of questions about the boundary between the world of information and the world of objects (not to mention the physical and social spaces in which they circulate).

Storage

Libraries, likewise, have never existed *eo ipso*, dropped as it were from the brow of Zeus; rather, they are urged into becoming by dint of norms, customs, regulations, and codes that reduce everywhere to history. They have always been more than mere storage-houses where documents are kept. They were, and remain, places of communion and conversation between the living and the dead; sites for gathering, reading, disputation, and teaching; spaces of exhibition and display, shelter and retreat. They have also always been places where the craft of writing is wedded to the arts of the scroll, the codex, and the book: places where the task of shaping words and thoughts interacts with modes of physical making and the distribution of materials in space, where process and product stand in uneasy, uncanny apposition.

Once temples reserved for a clerisy, once scarce and inaccessible places of refuge, libraries proliferated and underwent a wholesale democratization in the course of the nineteenth and twentieth centuries. The process was driven by the spread of literacy, the industrialization of printing, and the explosion in printed records of ever more heterogeneous kinds. The size and scale of libraries adapted to these expanded needs. In the process, the library became what it remains in the collective imagination today: namely, a vast storage container for printed matter, organized around a standardized classification system, to ensure access, flanked by some ancillary support structures (a reference desk, a reading room, an exhibition area, a cataloging and processing backroom). The definition is crystallized by architectures, like those of the New York Public Library (NYPL) and Harvard University's Widener Library, where the stack system serves as a primary structural support for the entire edifice.[2] When NYPL was under construction, it was this load-bearing system that elicited the public's wonderment:

> It is just completed, this marvelous network of steel bars and uprights, and exemplifies the very latest methods and appliances for the shelving of books [...] Above it will be placed the spacious reading room of the library, on either side the various halls, offices, and exhibition rooms. Thus surrounded, this monster bookcase becomes, architecturally, the heart of the whole structure, the treasure for whose protection this marble palace is built.[3]

Here was an abode literally built out of and on top of millions of books: at once a monstrous monument to the explosive growth of print and a sublime emblem of social and technological progress.

The information age started chipping away at the modern library's walls almost from the start. It transformed stack-centric libraries into data centers filled not only with books but also with workstation clusters, the deadly digital doubles of analog reading rooms. Initially tethered to local networks plugged into the digital catalogs stored on institutional servers, these dumb terminals were gradually opened up to the World Wide Web. In came a flood of access to new information and, with it, doubts about where a library begins and where it ends; about the library's ability to serve as a filter and guarantor of quality information; about the role of physical holdings, rather than services and activities, as the foundation stone of a library's sense of self. This identity crisis has come to a head with the increasing migration of documents to digital form; with the surge in e-publishing and e-booksellers; with the ubiquity of wireless networks; and with the exponential growth in on-line libraries, archives, collections, tools, and repositories.

Which brings us to our present threshold.

Activation

On the one side stand those who note that the world has be-come a library—or at the very least, that the World Wide Web has become a library. The library in question is already vaster than any physical library that has ever existed, and is growing rapidly. Open 24/7, it is available in any networked location, from the local coffee house to the bedroom to the city street to the classroom to the waiting room. It is also available on a pleth-ora of devices as small as the palm of a hand or as big as a me-dia wall. The library *qua* physical container, they reason, like an icehouse in the era of electric refrigeration, is a relic of the past.[4]

On the other side stand those who note, more often than not with a modicum of nostalgia, that libraries continue to perform pivotal civic, educational, and economic roles. Ac-cess to high-speed broadband networks is unevenly distribut-ed and nowhere a given. Library visits and usage statistics in the information age, rather than contracting, have grown. And the information explosion, far from serving the needs of the burgeoning knowledge economy, intensifies the need for quality information and expertise that libraries and librarians provide. In some colorations, this argument extends to one for the need for places of reflection and contemplation. It spills over into invectives against multitasking and pleas for forms of attention associated with surfaces that don't flicker, for long forms, for a renewed culture of concentration.

The present book argues neither position. It explores scenarios for the future of the library that presuppose the intermingling of the analog and the digital, books and e-books, paper and pixels. Media revolutions are about realignment, not substitution. Books are not about to go away. But many of the roles into which they settled during modernity's long reign (the monograph, the guidebook, the pamphlet, the textbook, the instruction manual, the comic book, to name a few) are undergoing significant shifts in function, material, production technique, distribution, and use. Printed books that appear superficially similar to those produced half a century ago are now digital in their design and production, their intellectual-property commitments, and the peritextual nimbus of "likes" and "favorites" they attract in social media.

Letterpress editions and *livres d'artiste* notwithstanding, these born-digital, abundantly networked tomes are put to old and emergent uses, configuring the cultural terms of authorship and reading in novel ways. Just think of the proliferation of mass-market puzzle books, especially those published in the wake of the explosion in popularity of the Japanese puzzle form Sudoku: bestseller tables in the large chain bookstores groan with stacks of these books under dozens of titles (*Sudoku for Artists, Kakuro for Lovers, Puzzles for the Ninety-Nine Percent*), many of them "authored" by the same person (or logarithm). Even by the generous criteria of games and puzzles, such books are hardly "authored" in any canonical or normative sense to which we were accustomed. And they are neither alone nor unprecedented. Mass-market genres with algorithmically-generated contents and easy re-intermediation into other print and electronic forms are proliferating much as, between 1910 and 1930, the Stratemeyer Syndicate produced hundreds of 50-cent tales of Tom Swift or Lyle Kenyon Engel's Book Creation, Inc. churned out hundreds of pseudonymously authored books for series such as The Kent Family Chronicles and Stagecoach during the 1970s. Which is not to say that there ever was a single kind of authorship. If book history teaches us anything (and it has taught much), it brings to life an awareness that authorial qualities are ever-shifting, manifold, contradictory, and everywhere materially manifest. Books that look like books of old are put to new uses, while new media serve in places where books once stood and dead media rumble back to life in new and unanticipated circumstances.

Books are being remediated, to be sure. Cherished norms are everywhere being put to question. Are books strictly entities with beginnings, middles, and ends? (Have they ever have been?) Is the page a meaningful or necessary narrative-graphic unit? (It wasn't for much of Western literary history.) Must one read left to right and top to bottom? (Do we ever really do so?) Are books always things made by authors? (No, nor have they been.) And is authorship a clearly-recognizable form of life (uncanny upwelling indeed: for authorship—of tweets and blog posts, of social-media personae—is alive and well, albeit in much different configurations)? At the same time, imaginal and aesthetic applications of the book to which we're accustomed—novels, memoirs, anthologies of stories and poems—respond to and rely upon practices, experiences, and networks of human relations, which are themselves undergoing transformation in the context of multiple, imbricated networks.

Writing of the compound of solitude and connection that constituted his experience of authorship in the first century BC, Catullus evokes the fraught exchange of creation and communication in terms that seem fresh today:

> To whom shall I give this pretty new treatise
> just polished with dry pumice?

Icebox – a gummy translucent cube equipped with lithium batteries and packed with wifi jammers, the Icebox is an inverted boombox that sucks up ambient signals and sounds, creating a local area network-free zone. When the librarian strolls in an Ice Box in hand, the law of the land is off-line. (BB, JS)

To you, Cornelius—for you used to be willing
to think something of my scribbling.
Even as you alone sought in three stages
to unfold the Italians' ages:
learned, by Jove, and laborious!
Therefore take this little opus
for whatever it's worth, o patron muse—
may it last more than one generation of use.[5]

The savor of solitary labor, the humble submission before time's vast power, the plaintive seeking after a connection with a reader, known or unknown, born or as-yet-unborn—such experiences are as recognizable to the blogger as they were to the ancient Greek or Roman poet. (If the author died with poststructuralism, she was reborn in 1999 with the release of Blogger.) At the same time, people are moved to draw their stories out of a roiling stew of richly networked, broad-ly-shared, consensually mass-hallucinatory media: an experi-ence with many effects, not all of them obvious or fully drawn, which renders fuzzy the boundaries of work, genre, and autho-rial identity that shaped normative presumptions in times past. The would-be author exists in a world of proliferating design and auto-design; of codecs, changelogs, diff pages, and notifi-cations; of mechanized, proliferating, animated, remote-control *amour-propre*.[6] What is the individual, the author-in-process, who exists at the nexus of these networks? For however much we conceive of cyberspace as space, it's a fiction organized around the cyber, the gubernatorial I. Technology thinker James Bridle captures this condition thusly:

This individualization effect is seen at every level of
technology, from the dot which places each of us at the
center of the digital map, up to the robot sensor networks

> which rely on a codified abstract of the world to guide
> them, rather than the truth on the ground: the map indeed
> becomes the territory.… in the glitches and unicode
> characters of printed database commands and international
> shipping labels, an underlying structure is made visible, the
> horsemeat scandal of information systems.[7]

Of course, these shifts are nowhere totalizing and altogether effacing. Manifestos notwithstanding, history doesn't work quite that way. A revolution becomes a renascence; an *eschaton* turns into efflorescence. Old ways well up in uncanny transposition, and even those forms that seem most resistant to change are reconfigured. As we catalog some of the current disruptions, it's important to remember that none of the material, functional, and cultural affordances of books have ever been fixed and immutable. In retrospect, formats and means of production superimpose in convincing complication. Every book is a palimpsest. The history of books is a palimpsest made up of palimpsests. And yet the scrolls of the libraries of Alexandria, or the codices in the abbey library of St. Gall, or the print artifacts in the British Library at the turn of the last century, are as different from one another as each is from the books found in our libraries today.

So were the libraries that contained them.

Architectonics

We promised the library *beyond* the book, meaning *beyond* in a bibliographically transcendent sense: the *bibliotheca* considered outside and even against the books it contains, with *volumen*, text, or tome as a black-boxed pretext for bringing together information-laden forms of life. Libraries as sites for access, congregation, contemplation, delight, discovery, dispute, escape, hiding, repose, research, secrecy, self-abnegation… a capacious cartography of qualities, which register their historical texture, weave in and out and among one another, just as much as do the forms of the book.

Of this shifting cast of qualities, storage has remained one of the more fixed and reliable. Whatever forms books take, however we imagine the institutions that frame them for us, holding, keeping, storing, and preserving are reliable standards by which being-library may be recognized. The standard modern definition brings us back to the etymology of the ancient Greek work for library, *bibliotheca*, which knots together the container and the contained.

The Bibliotheca as *theca*: a case for what? For all the things that are the case? What can the case be said to contain in the digital era? an era in which digital records may be exploding, but printing continues to chug along, churning out increasing quantities of records as well—or more precisely, where there exists a proliferation built also upon ever-increasing forms of redundancy, much of which is multiply versioned, channeled, and networked. Vast and stable legacies of the era of print are with us to stay. The custodianship of this past will remain an abiding task. Yet even these legacy materials have their digital editions and emendations. In what ways can the library be said to contain them? What is within and what is without, if I can carry or access a library one thousand times bigger than the entire library of Alexandria on the mobile device in my pocket? If the world itself is a library, what is the world *of* the library? Does it possess doors, windows or walls, book shelves, reference desks or reading rooms?

The world-making properties of the library—the *theca* as microcosm—are enduring facets of its container function. It

Central Parkbrary – existing kiosks, sheds, and utility buildings within a city park are redeveloped as an archipelago of specialized libraries dedicated to site-specific topics: landscape history, botany, park design, and local history. The greenhouse becomes a lending herbarium and plant library. The park itself serves as outdoor reading room. (JS)

was a quality that animated the institutional life of the Alexandrian libraries, as illustrated in Strabo's famous account:

> All [the buildings] are connected to each other and to the
> harbor and what lies outside the harbor. The Museum is
> also part of the royal complex. It has a walkway [*peripatos*]
> and an exedra and a great building that houses the place
> where the *philologoi* who take part in the Museum dine
> in common. Property, too, is held in common by this
> assembled group, and at their head is the priest who is put
> in charge of the Museum, who used to be appointed by the
> kings, but now by Caesar [Augustus]. Another part of the
> royal complex is the so-called *Sōma*. This is an enclosure
> where the tombs of the kings and of Alexander are located.[8]

Strabo's description of the *Museion*, the temple of the Muses also known as the Library of Alexandria, confirms that libraries have always been institutions built upon a paradox. On the one hand, they are places of enclosure: fortified bastions; sites of burial and storage of treasures; places of retreat from the din of the marketplace; sacred precincts and temples devoted to contemplation and prayer; self-sufficient worlds where, like their monastic descendants ten centuries later, a community of insiders, the priest and his retinue of *philologoi*, or lovers of the word, hold court. On the other hand, libraries open up *onto* the world: the noise of the street invades their sacred precinct; their collections cannot be built up without connections between capital and periphery in the form of trade routes; connections between society at large and communities of learning, like the priest and *philologos*. The world did not suddenly grow busy in the twentieth century, or at the time of the Glorious Revolution, or even as a result of the invention of moveable type. Networks—and the *ennui*, fatigue, and frictions that accompany them—are comprehensive qualities throughout the history of civilization, which is the history of the city. The conditions against which the library is meant to serve as a buffer or a bastion are precisely the conditions out of which it arises. The library is a product and a critique of urban possibilities.

Two horizons open up: one anthropological, one architectonic.

The library is born as *a place of entombment* and the librarian as its priest. But in the world of ancient Alexandria, the dead don't sleep. Rather, they are more powerful, alive, and talkative than the living. In the library, their endurance and transcendence is both expressed and contained, and the library is both the sacred place from which they enforce their rule over the living, and the *theca*, the vessel that contains their energies, protecting street and agora from their stupefying charisma.

It's worth thinking through the ways in which the library has carried forward and catalyzed change in the meanings not only of reading, knowledge, and information, but the meaning also of the dead: the nature of their congress with the living, the proprieties they hold over our institutions of education, knowledge transmission, and cultural production. Death has always marked an epistemic as well as a material and an ontological boundary. Do we now need to ponder the ways in which information networks variously elide and enable new formulations of the mortuary functions of knowledge production? Digital forms of information expression, after all, are rarely "dead" in the same way as the written letters Socrates warns against in the *Phaedrus*.[9] In the form of software and digital data, written texts can do things in the world: make copies of themselves, generate new texts or numerical expressions, transmediate themselves into new graphic and material modalities. These agencies are expressive. They are authored in much the same way as stories of old—and yet they take up residence in and alter the world in ways different from recited, printed, or hand-written texts.

The library is both a cemetery and the livebrary: a place of intensified, deeper sociality and communion, a place of burial and mummification that equals a place of worship and constant renewal, reactivation, and conversation across the centuries. As the storage/entombment function of "the book" (as once understood) sets over the horizon, these activation functions again move to the fore: what are we going to do with all that space that was once devoted to storage in the form of stacks? What forms of conversation can or should we promote? What sorts of sites of conversation do we require or desire? The democratization of this once-enclosed world is one of the great conquests of the modern era, one that has unleashed social forces, spread expertise, given rise to a vastly enriched universe of knowledge forms, and defined a new set of civic and public functions for temples of learning. Yet what will happen if it should merge into a million other spaces, losing its distinctiveness?

The library is born as a container shaped by its contents. Like the tomb, its sacred meaning is intimately associated with the *Sōma*, the bodies that it houses. The structure itself thus is summoned into being not along the lines of ideal or sacred geometries, not to serve the fulfillment of practical everyday tasks, but instead as the external manifestation of an internal treasure that needs, at once, to be manifest to the world of the living and protected, sheltered, locked up like a treasury or invisible reserve. Of course, the shape of those contents, the *Sōma*, at any point is a matter of not only the physical volumes, but also their projections into the social, the political, and the imaginal. Historically, the shape of that extended body, realized architecturally, has taken many forms—the mysterious grandeur of the gothic; the rough-hewn piety of the Romanesque; the Carnegie

Performance Librarian – Performance librarians tour the world putting on multimedia stage shows that weave together repositories, resources, and tools. The online communities they lead gather on the occasion of the shows and collaborate on the development of new reference tools. (AW, JK)

libraries' prim and simple classicism; the semi-translucent veined marble jewel box that is Yale's Beinecke library; the latticed curtain wall skin of Seattle Public with its cantilevered geometries. Today, those bookish projections also take material, technical, and expressive shape by way of networked iteration. The true façade of every library now opens out onto a (virtual) public square as big or small as the entire world. The treasures have been let out of the bag and have become ubiquitous; what sort of containers contain, store, and activate a *Sōma* such as this? Can architects be transformed into the librarian's natural friend rather than his or her "natural enemy," as Charles C. Soule argued in his 1891 "Points of Agreement Among Librarians as to Library Architecture," giving up the pursuit of grand effects and monumentalism in the name of service to functionality, flexibility, and actual user needs?[10] Does it even make sense to think of a single container type, rather than of a plurality of separate containers purpose-built to perform ever increasingly plural operations of bodying forth outside of the framework of any unifying structure? Does a new millennium of *libraries* lie beyond the millennia in which The Library was one?

It's this dichotomy—contents and container, text and apparatus, data and metadata, book and cover—that has long been elaborated and elided in the architectonic *Sōma* referred to as a library. Where does the book end and the library begin? Collections of texts take many forms, after all, and not all of them are libraries in the ordinary sense of the word. The Code of Hammurabi, for instance, is much older than the library at Nineveh; its corpus of 282 laws is the not the oldest legal charter, but the earliest complete one that has survived. It is known chiefly from a stele, carved of dark, close-grained volcanic rock, which resides today in the Louvre. Standing two and a quarter meters tall, the stele is a kind of archive insofar as its laws are not spun from theory or divine man-

Creative Incubators – soundproofed glass enclosures are placed in the library's lobby to house creative residencies of 6-12 months. Residents include writers working on books, media artists needing studio space, craft print shops, and non-profit groups. Each curates an installation that documents their research process. (JK, JS)

date, but from precedent. The code reflects a common-law tradition developed from a selection of Hammurabi's wise judgments in specific cases (the king billed himself as a "protector of the oppressed"—a quality that's hard to glimpse among the harsh judgments he meted out against slaves and women). Phrased in the form of conditional "if/then" statements (characteristic of latter-day code of another kind), this record of rulings had the force of law; and its monumental inscription must be understood not only as an accessible documentary copy of the law, but as part of its very ratification, enactment, and enforcement. The law acted its power by being public, by being monumental; this was not a record filed away in baskets to be taken out and consulted by scholars (although copies of the law were also rendered in clay tablets and filed in libraries). It's worth noting that the stele is carved in the shape of a great index finger—an executive appendage, to be sure, but the reader's searching digit as well.

Another gesture tying libraries together across time, one that arguably precedes the container function, is acquisition. "To author" is to compose, whether the composition takes the form of a single discrete text or many; to acquire, on the other hand, even if only a single text, is to make a library. (Of course, we also "author" by acquiring tropes and figures, but only rarely are these sub-rosa entanglements valorized as acquisition.) In a Mesopotamian library, like the library collected under the ruler Ashurbanipal at Nineveh in the seventh century BC, clay tablets with their pierced, kiln-hardened cuneiform were placed in baskets or encircled with twine and tied together into fascicles: gestures not only of gathering but of acquiring, holding, and keeping. Ashurbanipal's library contained some twenty-five thousand tablets of clay gathered in this way—acquired, contained, controlled. This gesture of acquisition is a metonym, the Mesopotamian ruler's *modus operandi* and *rai-*

son d'être. This is how literary behavior bodied forth institutionally in the context of Mesopotamian civilization, and it remains a governing principle in the course of the library's long history.

Yet there is in the library something vast, something that always exceeds the acquisitive. In its combinatory potential, its ambivalence, its polyglot drift across time, the collection of texts quickly overbalances the ambitions and intentions of its keeper. (In this, at least, acquisition is very much like authorship.) Throughout the history of libraries, the acquisitive mandate has supported, informed, and even been contradicted by an evolving typology of methods, affordances, and social arrangements: tool-like configurations of people and text using one another to make and do things.

For purposes of projecting possible library futures, it's worth identifying and describing a few of these configurations of what libraries can or could do and be. We're not going to catch all of them; nor are we going to exclude explosions of The Library into libraries, whether in the form of spin-offs or split-offs or novel ways of reorganizing the library's once predictable set of core organs. The configurations are many; as they emerge in history, they tend to endure, finding new application in a given sociocultural situation. An institution often expresses more than one of them. And they are never found solely in libraries. We might start with the **Mausoleum**—a place where the dead reside and where we go to commune with them; a **Cloister**, for reflection, meditation, and contemplation in shared solitude and labors of research and renewal; the **Database**—a container for information that is classified, accessible, controllable, infinitely expansible; the sort of **Warehouse** that we are later going to dub the "Accumulibrary" where the willy-nilly proliferation of documents and stuff is rendered navigable thanks to computational supports and mechanical eyes; a **Material Epis-**

Stackhunter – networks of sensors and RFID-tagged books gamify the stack system. Teams of schoolchildren are provided with age-appropriate bibliographical missions. When the books being pursued are located and deposited at home base, the winning team receives an allocation of points for the next round. (JK, JS)

temology, where collocations and consanguinities among different kinds of knowledge are proposed, experimented with, and affirmed; and a series of library types untethered to collections, from **Mobile Vectors** to **Civic Spaces**, where public ties are forged and affirmed, to freestanding **Reading Rooms** as spontaneous, popular, and (often) insurrectionary responses to closed and controlled versions of all of the above.

The earliest libraries expressed the qualities of the Mausoleum and the Database most emphatically. As with the Code of Hammurabi, the very act of recording in written form in an enduring medium—physical hardness and durability are etymological bedfellows—was a kind of commemoration for the ages, a scheme to embody time in material form; the connection of writing to the dead, to ancestors, to the numinous, fascinated the first writing cultures. Annals of empire, records of successful campaigns and major accomplishments, likewise served as epitaphs. To rummage through the library in search of these records, associating them with one another, remains down to this day an act of commemoration, of collected recollection. To stand on the shoulders of giants, in the famous formulation credited to Isaac Newton, is also to stand before their graves, their memorials, in communion with both their memory and their tangible traces.[11] Nowhere do the dead shoulder into our world more forcibly than in the stacks of a library.

Learned libraries of the ancient world incorporated spaces for contemplation, a feature the medieval cloister would refine. In the Hellenic world, learning also expressed an oral and peripatetic character; even as sizeable book collections grew at Alexandria, Pergamum, and Rhodes, it was by walking and talking, as well as by reading, that knowledge was understood to grow. This perhaps is the foundation of Socrates's suspicions regarding writing expressed (and problematically evoked by techno-utopians with alarming frequency) in the *Phaedrus*. It's worth noting that these sensory and kinesthetic modalities hardly disappeared with the spread of writing; rather, the convivial modes were incorporated into lettered learning. Alexandria's *Museion* featured an open colonnade—perhaps evoking Plato's legendary haunt, the grove of Academe—to serve as contemplation's requisite temple. In such a space, readers not only accessed the dead evoked by the library's books, but found the energetic quiet that animates the speculative modes of gazing upon the world that the ancient Greeks understood as *theoria* (θεωρία). Likewise, in ancient Rome, libraries adorned private villas, but were also available at the public baths, a crucial space for civic making in a republic whose citizenry struggled to come to grips with imperial ambition.[12] (When they gathered in unprecedented numbers two millennia later, in the libraries of the nineteenth-century western world, books would again provide these civic environments to their readers, in the form of the public library movement.)

As the ancient world fragmented, learning retreated into quiet pockets of safety. The cloister model was pioneered by Cassiodorus, the sixth-century divine who founded the *Vivarium* [place of life], named for the fish ponds that fed the cenobitic monks who took up residence at his estate. Cassiodorus's *Institutiones*, the great dark-age epistemological work, organized the world's knowledge into sacred and secular, ordering the latter in the form the liberal arts would take in the middle ages, as mundane support and enablers for theological learning. A model for the world, Cassiodorus's scheme seems poignant now—a supremely ordered scheme of knowledge, secreted away in a cloistered haven from the energies of a world falling apart. As the greatest cloister library, the Biblioteca Apostolica Vaticana, grew in size and complexity in the late middle ages, its custodians, too, would seek to bring its books under a measure of control. In this

Bookscout — a book in every cluster of stacks has been programmed so that, when a patron picks it up, it transforms itself into a navigational device, lighting up a family of fifty related books. The relations are tuned according to prior patterns of use, and affinities that range from thematics to typesetting to a user's history. (JS)

they followed the rough model offered by Cassiodorus half a millennium before, dividing the books into sacred and secular mansions, with further divisions in a hierarchy extending from the Bible to canon law on the sacred side, and from philosophy to poetry on the secular. This ordered collection presented readers with a materialized epistemology, an idealized model of learning, a *mappa mundi* of mundane knowledge.

During the Chartist uprisings in Britain in the mid-nineteenth century, activists organized reading rooms to offer laborers a means for education and self-improvement. In turn-of-the-century New York, children's librarians lent whole boxes of books to young people with the expectation that they would take them home and spread them among the family, while mule-drawn traveling libraries, the forerunners of late twentieth-century bookmobiles, delivered bibliophily to rural communities. These landlocked collections shared something too with ship's libraries—trunks of salt-speckled volumes that roamed the high seas. These were instant libraries of a kind—arising in specific locales to meet ephemeral needs. They expressed the curious property of books to domesticate space, to enact in vagrant and peregrinatory conditions the whole typology limned above—turning a fo'c'stle of a ship into a cloister, a prairie cabin into a place to commune with the long-departed, a tenement flat into a model of the knowledge of the world.

Mausoleum, **Cloister**, **Database**, **Warehouse**, **Material Epistemology**, **Mobile Vector**, **Civic Space**, and **Instant Reading Room**—in the sections that follow we present a series of forward-looking, historically informed, speculative sketches of these basic types. We're trying to work our way toward a kind of pattern language (to borrow from the architect and city planner Christopher Alexander) for the library beyond the book—where, again, *beyond* means *beside* or *outside* or *orthogonal* to—elaborated in a probe of the interstices between anthropology, literature, history, architecture, and design.[13] Our sequence of types is organized along chronological lines (but is not a timeline). It begins with models of the library that are built around devotion to deep time; it then moves on to consider libraries that variously balance the competing demands of serving history and the present; it concludes with models that stress service to the here and now.

For all its variety, every position within this cluster of definitions of the library is meant to pick up on some of the qualities that people have sought in libraries past and present, regardless of the media contained, and to translate such qualities into contemporary terms. Thus, in assembling the present pattern book, we've settled on those that have special resonance and application in the context of a networked world where the physical and the virtual, the offline and the online, are intertwined with increasing intimacy. Like the worlds that preceded it, ours is not without its paradoxes. Today we long for information at our fingertips, but our fingertips derive greater pleasure from the feel of fine paper, cloth, leather, or wood than from the touchscreens that are our devoted servants and companions. We prize solitary reading and study, but still long for the company of fellow readers and students as we do so. We dream of infinite libraries that tag along with us in our pockets everywhere that we go, while yearning for the stately sense of communion that only the grand reading halls of yore seem ready or able to provide.

This book makes no claim that its library types are the only ones pertinent to the present epoch; nor ought they to be considered in isolation. Indeed, they have often been mixed and matched in the past—and we consider remix the most encompassing and plausible future scenario. It constitutes an effort to give that remix an initiatory spin and to plant some seeds for thought in the process. It's neither a white paper on the problems facing libraries today nor a policy manual for digital era librarians nor an idea book for library architects and designers nor a collection of maps, like R. David Lankes's *The Atlas of New Librarianship*, intended to provide guidance to librarians as they navigate uncharted information-age waters.[14] Less a conventional scholarly book than a *library* of case studies, scenarios, ideas, anecdotes, and quotations, it invites the reader to assemble its component parts and to think hard.

So here are the instructions for assembly. You reached this point in the essay that forms the book's backbone via a prefatory cartoon that recounts the steampunk saga of Melvil Dewey's time travels. Continue to read the book oriented in the standard manner and you'll go on to experience the rest of the essay. Rotate it counterclockwise ninety degrees to skim the thought experiments (Provocations) that flicker along its margins. Some are practical; others speculative; others are flights of fancy. At the essay's one-quarter point, a sequence of windows—micro-essays on the basic fittings of libraries, their past and future—intrudes and provides an intermezzo between the opening section that you are about to complete and the scenarios plus conclusion that await you. Next come the notes and credits followed by an afterthought entitled *Cold Storage*.

Cold Storage takes the reader on a journey into the heart of one, otherwise invisible, iteration of what a research library is today: a world of storage stacks built for use by machine intelligences and sensor systems working in the service of a large community of voracious readers. The location is Harvard but, as is the case with each of the locally drawn examples scattered across the pages of the present book, "Harvard" could be "Nearly Anywhere."

Welcome to the Library (beyond the book).

Book

It's an icon and a receptacle, a paragon and a provider. The Symbolist poet Stéphane Mallarmé once wrote that "everything in the world exists to give rise to a book." But what do we actually know about the ideal *form* that the book should take? Normative propositions dissolve in a haze of historical variations and exceptional cases. Books, after all, have been clay slabs and long rolls of silk or papyrus; in the synagogue, the ideal form remains the scroll, fashioned from parchment and richly appointed. The codex, which cradled the gospels, is a form factor that accommodates precious manuscripts and mass-market paperbacks with equal aplomb. In this, what until recently seemed its final form, the book offered a remarkably resilient architectural pattern: a dependable navigational system running front to back and top to bottom; a body with a spine and a complete, complex anatomy; a haptic hinge opening the doors of contemplation; a portable, many-mansioned house for knowledge. And now, with the book emerging as a networked creature, its content con-

Reading Stand ("can be slid about the room alongside a chair, allowing for many postures"); *Illustrated Catalog* (Boston: Library Bureau, 1890), 146.

Common Sense Binder ("has made friends wherever tried"); *Classified Illustrated Catalog* (Boston: Library Bureau, 1899), 106.

tained in bytes and rendered in pixels, its wonted materiality seems to fade into abstraction. Long the scene of a solitary encounter with knowledge, the book may now be shared line by line, its readers' progress through the text tracked and analyzed, its contents scraped and remixed, its finitude and finality pried open. Yet books have long anticipated the "spime," Bruce Sterling's name for objects that are trackable through time and space. For in their margins, flyleaves, and interlinear notes, books have made room for a record of their dealings with us and with one another. Despite the strictures of page and binding, their edges have always leaked. In the library, books have tried out a series of evolutionary adaptations for beckoning, holding, and controlling their readers, from critical apparati that script their use to spine labels and title pages to clasps and chains to checkout cards and bibliographic database records. Long before barcodes, RFID tags, and MARC records, books were sending astral projections into the ether. Every book, in a sense, is already an e-book.

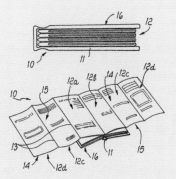

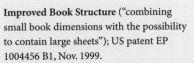

Improved Book Structure ("combining small book dimensions with the possibility to contain large sheets"); US patent EP 1004456 B1, Nov. 1999.

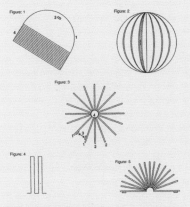

Metamorphic Book ("in an open form defines an object such as a plaything" like a ball); US patent EP 0635291 A1, July 1994.

Bookshelf

The history of shelving tracks closely alongside that of written records. Long before the *theca* became a **biblio***theca*, the shelf a **book**shelf, clay tablets were housed in lateral storage structures built against or into walls. They were eventually joined by papyrus scrolls, stacked like carpet rolls, their tagged ends poking outward. Later came wood tablets, codices, printed books. Vertical stacking remained the norm, displaced by horizontal arrays only when the spines of printed books became the standard locus for identifying marks. In the course of this history, the bookshelf remains an organizing unit: not a random dumping ground, but a place of ordering where, thanks to the actions of a keeper, *logoi* were brought into line with a single higher law. The book can serve only one master. Never a perfect unit but always a unit, a place where the infinite proliferation of meanings— read "plausible organizational

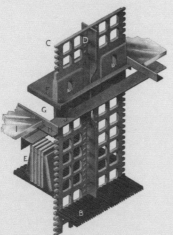

Isometric Drawing of 16" Stack ("permitting free circulation of air and moderate light"); *Book Stack and Shelving for Libraries* (Jersey City, NJ: Snead and Co., 1908), 41.

Door fitted with Section of Wall Stack, New York University Library; *Library Catalog – A Descriptive List* (Boston: Library Bureau, 1904), 41.

schemes"— is kept in check, the bookshelf becomes a master metaphor for the library itself: for the library as a (fragile) place of cohesion; for the publication series that, for all its diversity, enacts a plan; for an infrastructure that supports even the most fluid readerly desires.

Digital documents have no spine. They can be stacked as icons, lists, or blocks, in vertical, horizontal, orthogonal, 2d, and 3d arrays. They are born in a swarm of tags and, in the course of their lives, the swarm becomes a sea. And they can simultaneously live on the bookshelves of a legion of masters while taking up no space. The digital bookshelf returns, thus, as a realm both of comforting finitude and of infinite possibility, where local logics can be made no less present and palpable than they were in the tablet vaults of Sumerian Ebla, but open to the combinatory play of the hive mind.

Experimental Shelving Unit ("can be expanded from 300 to 3000 volumes [...] affordable to all social classes"); Friedrich Kiesler, *Manifeste du Correalisme*, 1947.

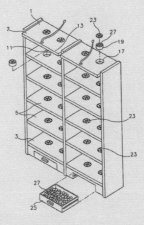

Multifunctional Bookshelf Structure ("comprising insecticide, dehumidifier, deodorizer and aromatics"); EP 1297763 B1, Oct. 2001.

Card Catalog

Still one of the furnishings most closely associated with the library in popular consciousness, the card catalog is also one of its most ephemeral appurtenances. For centuries it was rare for collections to consist of more than a few hundred books tidily cataloged in simple lists. Even the holdings of the Library of Alexandria could be reduced to the 120 tablets of the *Pinakes*, composed by the poet Callimachus in the third century BCE. By the late eighteenth century,

however, printed works had become commodities. Libraries and scholars traded books in bulk. Men like Edward Gibbon, the author of *The History of the Decline and Fall of the Roman Empire*, began to create the first modern card catalogs for their growing libraries, noting authors and titles on the backs of playing cards. By the middle of the next century, exasperated librarians were cutting up the old full-page shelf lists and sorting them into "slip catalogs" that could be reshuf-

Hammond Card Cataloger ("for catalog-cards, shelf-lists, bulletins, and correspondence"); *Classified Illustrated Catalog* (Boston: Library Bureau, 1899), 158.

Small Tray Outfit with 6 Trays ("for the beginner of a card catalog, business list or index"); *Classified Illustrated Catalog* (Boston: Library Bureau, 1897), 48.

fled on the fly to accommodate the torrent of books produced by the steam-powered press. Although he did not invent the card catalog, Melvil Dewey cemented its place in the library world. His Decimal Classification System, which ordered all knowledge into ten distinct categories, was supremely well-tailored for the card-catalog system. Librarians could shuffle their vast decks of cards into faceted suits: jack of authors, queen of subjects, king of titles. But as the facets of knowledge began to multiply geometrically, fractally, the card catalog found itself as out of step as the Tarot, as superannuated as pinochle. Today, the cards have migrated into digital records bearing a train of increasingly complex metadata; and these, in turn, are being multiplied by crowdsourced and user-generated tagging. Catalogs interconnect. The card game is played on a multidimensional table.

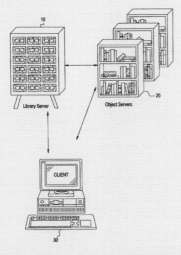

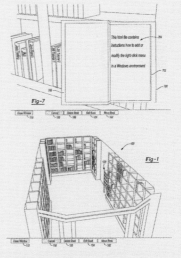

Dividing, mapping, and storing large digital objects in library system ("by division into smaller pieces, limitations regarding size are avoided"); US patent 5857203 A, July 1996.

Virtual Library File System ("displays virtual book objects [on] a plurality of virtual shelves"); US patent 20080216009 A1, March 2008.

Carrel

The carrel belongs to a universe of furnishings that include the lectern, bookstand, writing table, and pew. Its origins are monastic, rooted in the *carula*, the cloister-housed study nook. The modern carrel is the *carula*'s secular descendant. Stripped of ornament, chained scriptures, and mantles of privilege, it is a document processing station for the age of critical reason. Designed for use rather than ownership, the carrel is a desk that favors sorting, reading, and note-taking operations rather than personal storage and filing. Temporary constellations of knowledge march across its surfaces, one after another, en route toward publications, potential or actual, that loom

The Bibliomaniac ("this one pleasoure haue I/ Of bokes to haue grete plenty and aparayle/ I take no wysdome by them"); Sebastian Brandt, *The Ship of Fools*, (Edinburgh: William Paterson, 1874).

Folding Reading Desk ("when reference to different authorities and subjects is frequently required"); US patent 317,288, May 1885.

invisibly over the horizon. Few will find readers or have hundred-year lives; most will fade into the night sky, like fireworks. The carrel's role as a microcosm of retreat and enclosure within the macrocosm of the library is evolving toward interactive redesigns. The scenarios are multiple: the carrel as curation station whose marching digital and physical constellations are broadcast to library patrons; the modular carrel that can be isolated or assembled into islands; the carrel as classroom; the carrel as multimedia production studio. Retreat and enclosure will remain an integral part of this future, but in the company of designs for advance and disclosure.

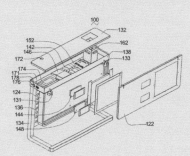

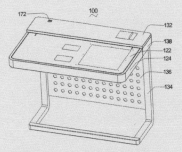

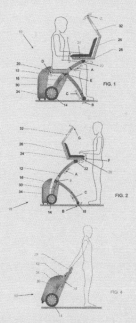

Vehicle-mounted library workstation (antenna-equipped book and card identifying module with RFID tag readers for loans); US Patent 20130112725 A1; June 6, 2012.

Mobile computer workstation ("luggage trolley with storage area for mobile dialogue device and seat element"); US Patent EP 2409599 B1, March 2, 2011.

Copy Station

Copy derives from the Latin *copia* and long denoted a bounty that was the stuff only of dreams. Texts were scarce before Gutenberg, so study meant three C's: Copy, Collect, and Collate. Every medieval library was surrounded by cells with copyists. Some contained a dedicated scriptorium: a workshop replete with folios, quills, brushes, inkpots, rulers, knives, and tables. By the fourteenth century, copying began to migrate out of the cloister into nearby shops overseen by the modern librarian's ancestor, the *librarius*, and his stationer double, the *stationarius*. Together they were responsible for the transcription, keeping, rental, and selling of books to a new class of copyists: university students. Practices of copying changed little over the course of the next six centuries: centuries during which the spread and, subsequently, industrialization of printing gave rise to so great a proliferation of printed matter that the word *copy* came to assume connotations of cheapness and theft. The advent of electrostatic duplication marks the beginning of a transformation brought to term when photocopiers marched into offices in the mid-twentieth century.

Hectographs ("a simple method of making up to 100 copies of any matter"); *Illustrated Catalog* (Boston: Library Bureau, 1890), 138.

Mimeograph ("it gives matter an autographic character not obtainable from type"); *Illustrated Catalog* (Boston: Library Bureau, 1890), 139.

Initially unwelcome due to fears regarding damage to bindings and copyright, soon they had invaded libraries as well. Copying was now a labor-intensive activity carried out in segregated do-it-yourself versions of the nineteenth century printing shop, characterized by heat, mechanical noise, and exposure to ink dust and chemicals. Freed from the burdens of rote transcription, note taking could evolve into an extension of thinking. The core unit of the photocopy was not the phrase but instead the page qua visual unit. Collation was redefined as the assemblage, cutting, pasting, and marking of photocopied pages. The same constellation of practices has carried over into the era of scanning with one major shift: OCR has brought words, sentences, and paragraphs back within the compass of the copyist's labor, in the process renewing medieval worries regarding accurate transcription. Today, the copy room has become a relic. Scanners, copiers, and recorders are in the pockets of every reader. The copy shop is everywhere, from the stacks to the streets.

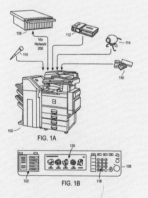

FIG. 1A

FIG. 1B

Document collection manipulation ("the order in which documents are presented dictates the organization of the stored collection"); US Patent 7757162 B2, Oct. 15, 2003.

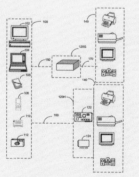

Smart phones that support voice activated commands ("the user may issue voice commands to stream, send, play, print, or display digital content"); US Patent 20130109353 A1, Dec. 10, 2012.

Librarian

In antiquity, the librarian was a *custos librorum*, a keeper of books—a caretaker, guard, and amanuensis. From antiquity through the early modern era, they were loosely-specified generalists—makers as well as keepers of books, teachers as well as providers of instructional materials. And they were more or less exclusively male. Librarians in the late nineteenth century were energized with a sense of movement. As steam-driven presses multiplied the number of printed books geometrically, the problems of acquiring, maintaining, and helping readers to find their way multiplied as well. In response to social disruptions of the industrial age librarians defined readers as clients in need of guidance and service. Teaching, access, and assimilation became watchwords to replace the conservative, custodial energies of old. Branch service was born, and the neighborhood library became a liminal space where the foreign-born poor could bootstrap themselves in settlement-house visions of an emancipated working class. In the course of these changes, librarianship was recoded as a role for women to play—

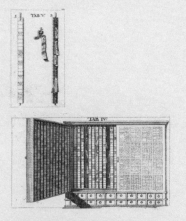

Scrinium Literatum (3000 alphabetically ordered headings can be contained in this mobile note closet); Vincent Placcius, *De arte excerpendi* (Stockholm, 1689), 152-53.

Vertical Filing Cabinet ("this practical construction is familiar to all librarians"); *Classified Illustrated Catalog* (Boston: Library Bureau, 1900), 113.

increasing the professional opportunities for women while also restricting its agencies according to the normative expectations of a patriarchal society. In the context of networked information, librarianship looks less and less like a profession with perks and prescriptions, and more of a sensibility. In a sense, then, we're all librarians now. And yet the role still has a vital future as a profession and vocation. The networks that deliver information—which include the internet, but also physical and social infrastructure of all kinds—function best in the context of participation.

Librarians foment and facilitate such participation, helping citizens to forge their own connections with the life of information. The overlapping systems and infrastructures combine in complex and surprising ways, requiring multiple intelligences to disentangle. Where librarians once acted as gatekeepers guarding limited resources, they now become lock-pickers and safecrackers. What they guard instead is our very participation in information culture: our opportunity, our privacy, and our freedom.

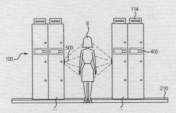
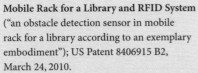

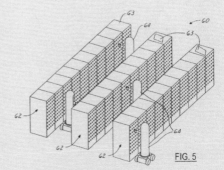

Mobile Rack for a Library and RFID System ("an obstacle detection sensor in mobile rack for a library according to an exemplary embodiment"); US Patent 8406915 B2, March 24, 2010.

Data Library System Having Movable Robotic Librarian ("the system includes a robotic librarian operable for moving about the data library"); US Patent 6801834 B1, Feb. 4, 2003.

Library Card

The library card is a passport to a world in which access to libraries has been democratized and the lending of books confirms their civic vocation. Its double is the circulation record. It anoints the bearer as a citizen or citizen-in-the-making pledged to treat every book as an expression of the *res publica*. The library card is born a minimalist. At most, it displays a name, address, number, expiration date, and library seal. An ancestor of the wallet-sized credit card, it initially assumes the form of an embossed surface that prints under the pres-

Automatic Electric Charging Machine ("absolute accuracy, speedy charging of books, no lost books, no arguments"); *Gaylord Triangle* (March 1939), 4.

Addressograph-Multigraph Printer and Plates ("characters can be printed on any document as often as required"); Thomas Landau, *Library Furniture and Equipment*, (London: Crosby/Lockwood, 1963), 16.

sure of rollers or frottage. These dumb beginnings as a meager press forme have not been overcome through the addition of barcodes or magnetic strips. But the library card is about to get smart. "Smart" means biometric forms of identification; the ability to carry a reader's entire history of searches, loans, and scans; use for payment of special services; interoperability across institutions; a social fingerprint capable of tapping into the bearer's broader network of interests. The library card of the future will be born a maximalist.

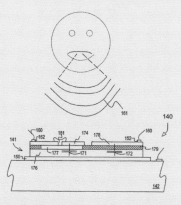

Voice activated smart card ("for applications such as identification, command execution, encryption, and speech recognition"); US Patent 8266451 B2, Aug. 31, 2001.

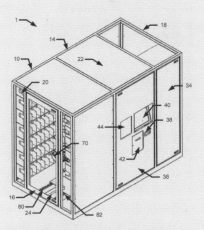

Automated library ("unit containing slots to hold digital and print media; a programmable robot; a patron interface panel"); US Patent 20110231007 A1, March 21, 2011.

Reference Desk

While the need for systems of reference extends back to the colophons etched on the backs of clay tablets, the modern reference desk is a product of the industrial age. It presupposes libraries on a scale beyond the physical and mental grasp of individuals, a proliferation of specialized domains of knowledge, each with unique models of organization, and a concept of the library as a public resource serving the needs of society in which knowledge is understood as the engine of progress. Within this universe, the reference desk figures as much as an access point to locally housed collections as a hub for world-wide resources, tools, and systems. That hub is fixed at the library's center. It assumes the form of a temple within a temple whose robust walls are built out of folio-sized reference tomes. Its al-

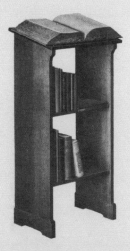

Pedestal Type Dictionary Stand ("most practical to hold a dictionary for reference use"); *Gaylord's Triangle* 9.11 (July 1930): 1.

Reference Desk and Reading Room with students studying at night (Chubb Library, Ohio University, circa 1950; CC 2.0 license).

tar is the reference desk itself: built for the ages but forever available to serve the cause of knowledge. Its priest is the reference specialist. Today, the temple's walls have vaporized into bits and bytes available on digital desktops and mobile devices. The library is everywhere and the reference oracle is a search box with algorithmically sorted results. The need for expertise has expanded, as a result.

But reference has become decoupled from the hub. The priest is now free to rove about the stacks and the world, summoned via instant message or microblog to the site where information is sought, produced, or shared. In the era of social media and networked communications, reference is self-reference: democratized, user-driven, user-centered.

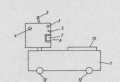

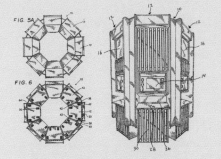

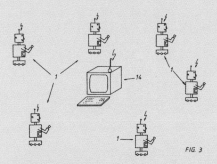

Information kiosk ("an interactive information source for multiple users, including in wheelchairs"); US Patent 5702166 A, June 9, 1995.

Computer-controlled system for reception and information desk ("for reception with multi-axis program and sensor-controlled robots"); US Patent EP 0958897 A1, April 1999.

Scenarios

Étienne-Louis Boullée, *Mémoire sur les moyens de procurer à la bibliothèque du Roi les avantages que ce monument exige*, engraving, 1785. Source: gallica.bnf.fr/Bibliothèque Nationale de France.

Living Mausoleum

In his prologue to the second book of *The Advancement of Learning* (1605), Francis Bacon writes:

> The works which concern the seats and places of learning

are four—foundations and buildings, endowments with revenues, endowments with franchises and privileges, institutions and ordinances for government—all tending to quietness and privateness of life, and discharge of cares and troubles; much like the stations which Virgil prescribeth for the hiving of bees:

> Principio sedes apibus statioque petenda,
> Quo neque sit ventis aditus, &c.[15]

The Virgilian verses are perhaps best translated "seek a stable home for your bees first that is sheltered from the wind" (*Georgics* 4.8-9), by which the Roman poet and his successor mean to underscore the fundamental value of a stable, secluded place of contemplation for the production of honey (= wisdom). Next comes a passage oft-cited in library apologetics:

> The works touching books are two—first, libraries, which
> are as the shrines where all the relics of the ancient
> saints, full of true virtue, and that without delusion or
> imposture, are preserved and reposed; secondly, new
> editions of authors, with more correct impressions, more
> faithful translations, more profitable glosses, more diligent
> annotations, and the like.[16]

Bacon's theme is not just preservation but also *advancement.* So the panegyric to libraries as shrines, often cited alone, is incomplete without the accompanying paean to editing, revision, and correction. The wording is meticulous: libraries are places of burial where saints, like Virgil, and relics, like the *Georgics*, are "reposed." But *repose* has two meanings. It designates the unperturbed sleep of the well-buried dead. It also designates the bee-like buzz of continuous posing: the process, forever carried out in the present, of stripping away delusions, impostures, and errors so as to arrive at "true virtue."

Bacon's two-pronged account of the library as shrine, or what we have dubbed the "living mausoleum," provides a useful antidote both to the excessive exuberance of techno-utopians promising an end to physical libraries and universal access to "all the world's information," and to the defensiveness of portions of the library-going public when confronted with reimaginings of the library's future (as in the case of the recent flap over the redesign of New York Public Library's flagship Fifth Avenue building). It also usefully asserts two core claims that have profoundly shaped the entire history of the library as an institution: namely, that the library is *an institution built upon deep time* and that devotion to deep time presupposes *a grand and enduring physical edifice.*[17]

Virgil's "beehive"/station unexposed to the wind is thus sheltered not just from the winds of the present but also from the sorts of contracted time scales that characterize weather events—read: markets, public opinion, fashion and fads, the whims of demagogues and tyrants, blindered vocationalism and narrow utilitarianism. The intertwined acts of preservation and production that libraries enable are of a different scale and order. They unfold not over days and weeks and years, but over centuries and millennia. The honey of wisdom is secreted slowly and steadily. When properly brought forth, it keeps for a very long time; perhaps even forever.

The shelter form required to ensure this long-term process of distillation, to honor and serve the sainted and to preserve their relics, to promote carefree study and worship, necessarily assumes the form of a monumental construction. In Latin, a *monumentum* is a commemorative record, statue, or fortress-like edifice that reminds, marks and warns, and in so doing, endures. In German the word is *Denkmal*: a "stimulus to thought" that combats the certainty of oblivion by means of supports, materials, and architectures that are built to last. In Russian, a monument is a *памятни*, a memory object or memorial. Monuments are mausolea inasmuch as their purpose is at once honorary and funerary: like the eponymous massive marble *Mausoleion*, once counted among the Seven Wonders of the Ancient World, erected in 353 BCE in Halicarnassus to enshrine the Persian satrap Mausolos. However designated, there is no more tradition-bound or conservative domain of construction, making, or inscription: tradition-bound in its recourse to stone as the material of memory-making and memory-marking; conservative in its reliance upon a standardized repertory of ornamental styles, geometrical forms, and conventions of classical derivation. Monuments are built to dazzle and to weather history's storms, to commune with the past and speak to the present and future in the voice of deep time.

The rise of vast online libraries and the migration of document forms into digital environments in no way "solves" the problem of deep storage and retrieval that Bacon's library as living mausoleum was designed to address. On the contrary, they radicalize the problem. Digital materials pose distinctive challenges that involve, among other things, their inherent fragility and volatility, software and platform dependencies, and bit rot. Such challenges are multiplied by the sheer volume of digital materials being produced and accumulated, as well as by the redundancy of significant portions of this data: a redundancy characterized not only by multiple versions and copies but also by overlaps between digital and print. The oldest digital files currently preserved date back less than half a century: a drop in the bucket with respect to the human record, not to mention geological time or the history of the cosmos. Digital preservation is in its infancy and remains something of a craft. Efforts can prove costly, particu-

Reading Taverns — the library's basement is transformed into a nocturnal reading room which hosts book-related social activities as well as performances, readings, and poetry slams. The Reading Tavern is the home for local literary clubs whose job it is to curate its nooks, crannies, tables, and benches. (1S)

larly at scale. So who will see to it that the most significant portions of the (digital) historical record will be available centuries from now? Who will ensure that not only "original" records are preserved but also the history of impressions, translations, glosses, and annotations—the centuries of buzz—that bring those records alive? How will this be done?

In the first instance, answers to such questions will come from familiar quarters: living mausolea dedicated to digital collecting, preserving, and production, much like the living mausolea that have made the era of print so remarkably successful from the standpoint of the accumulation, production, and dissemination of knowledge. In cases like those of institutions such as the Library of Congress, Deutsche Nationalbibliothek, Bibliothèque Nationale de Paris, the National Diet Library of Japan, or major university research libraries, the digital wing will become just another appendage within an already vast analog edifice (albeit one where screens and work stations outnumber parchment pages and wooden lecterns). The coexistence of heterogeneous media types has always been a defining feature of these traditional shrines of learning. Given that much of the human record is locked up in stone, clay, papyrus, parchment, and paper, not to mention in objects and physical sites, institutions where the digital and analog productively commingle are sure to remain fundamental to the advancement of learning.

By their very nature such institutions are additive and absorptive, tendentially "universal" in their collecting habits, but selective. When new media arise, they are rarely welcomed into the fold right away. Some never make the cut at all. But, once they have demonstrated their staying power or significance, they are gradually introduced into the circle of their more venerable predecessors, whether in shared spaces or separately. The reasons may be ideological; more often, ephemerality is at issue. Devotion to deep time translates into a set of minimum requirements for membership in a club that not all media can or should meet. (Hence the efflorescence of alternative and counter-structures—see our final tripartite scenario—that seek to document parts of the human record unlikely to find their way into living mausolea.)

Alongside such additive and absorptive all-encompassing structures, new types of specialized institutions are sure to arise as well: the digital descendants of venerable manuscript or print-era ancestors like the Folger Shakespeare collections, Chicago's Newberry, and the Plantin Moretus, dedicated to digital collections building, archeology, forensics, preservation, study, and analysis. Like their predecessors, most will specialize not in digital materials *tout court* but in distinctive eras or categories of materials and their supports: materials so "full of true virtue," as Bacon would have it, as to require the building of physical shrines where such relics are preserved and reposed in perpetuity. The collections of these new institutions will consist in data repositories stored on off-site server farms, software libraries, hardware devices, games and emulators of every stripe, and the like. Their hallways will be lined not with folio editions or pages from illuminated manuscripts but instead with exhibition cases containing early computer displays, input device prototypes, and tractor-feed printouts documenting seminal moments in the history of programming. Their seminar rooms will be hybrid spaces framed by video walls, allowing for real-time collaboration among scholars, whether physically co-present or tele-present or toggling between the two. Their reading rooms will be filled with curation stations that share with the on-site and on-line hive otherwise invisible actions of digital re-posing. Other rooms still will be outfitted like forensics labs, with damaged hard drives on examining tables, fat folders of printouts and analytics on

Labrary I – a library floor is transformed into a lab housing citizen science projects, each represented by a station with field equipment that can be tested, instructions and protocols for study, and a library of materials. The room houses weekly informational team meetings, coordinated with local schools. (JG, JK, JS, MB)

the shelves, and diagnostic tools scattered about. But they will also be equipped with virtual reading rooms where scholars are able to run data mining algorithms on the library's servers via virtual machine software. If the public façade of such institutions opens up onto the World Wide Web, physical co-presence in a community of expertise and a place tending to quietness will animate their core much like companies of monks enlivened medieval scriptoria. The relics of saints were always already multiples whose magic resided less in their claim to uniqueness than in their ability to catalyze the energies of a community as well as higher forces. Such will be the destiny of digital relics as well.

However novel or distinctive, many of the issues institutions dedicated to deep storage will confront, whether the universal or the specialized, have a familiar ring: constrained acquisition budgets; limitations in server rack space (instead of bookshelf space); high maintenance and personnel costs; the need for backups and vast libraries of emulators; light, temperature, and climate controls; fire and flood protection; safeguarding patron privacy; and security. If data assets are to be preserved for a posterity understood as deep time, selectivity will be required, which means a strategy for active accessioning as well as active deaccessioning. Also necessary will be tiered strategies for dealing with digital assets that make value judgments regarding what deserves full-court curation and processing, what can be treated in partial fashion, and what can be left unprocessed in deep storage, even at the risk of total loss. (The blanket application of a uniform standard long ago demonstrated its futility and continues to be responsible for processing logjams in the world of archives and special collections.) Among the additional implications is the need for a failsafe backup system for the most precious data assets. Perhaps these are printed out on archival paper, bound and placed in vast off-site storage structures "just in case." The scenario has a steampunk ring to it. But print is highly stable and relatively low cost, and from a long duration standpoint, any preservation model that presupposes the survival of a given network architecture, a set of functioning devices, server farms, and the existence of the electrical grid, leaves something to be desired. So why not consider analog backup systems to digital data?[18]

By summoning up this vision of living digital mausolea appended (or not) to the great pre-print and print-era living mausolea of the modern era, our aim is to underscore the degree to which the analog/digital opposition begins to dissolve when service to *deep time* is embraced as the library's core mission. Libraries devoted to long-term knowledge accumulation, preservation, and activation, from the libraries of Alexandria to modern descendants like the British Library, represent what is perhaps the most enduring answer to the question of "what is a library?" But, however much access has been democratized, they remain bastions of privilege and exception almost by definition: holies of holies, shrines to the ancients and their remains, places of pilgrimage, designed for study, fellowship, and visitation. To invoke them as models for libraries of all kinds and on all scales, as if they were the unifying trunk of a many branched typological tree, seems increasingly implausible in the wake of two centuries of transformative events: from the industrialization of printing and the rise of public libraries and educational institutions to the advent of digital libraries on the World Wide Web. The very complexity and pervasiveness of today's world of information would seem to argue, instead, for a multiplication and diversification of library identities and types. Or so runs the argument of the following pages devoted to sketching out diverse scenarios for future libraries or library-like institutions.

Media Memory Palace — a hall is dedicated to collecting working examples of devices from the prior history of computing, media, and communications. They allow patrons to practice manual typewriting, early word processing, shadowbox photography, film splicing on old editing tables. Hackathons are held to promote the production of anachronistic multimedia experiments. (JS)

The chime generator integrated into the Clock of the Long Now, Long Now Museum, San Francisco, CA; photograph by Todd Lappin, July 12, 2008; CC license 2.0.

Neocloister

Retreat, reading, and reflection are habits long associated with one another, a mutually-reinforcing triad of states and norms associated with the library as place of research. In ideal, each one feeds and supports the others. The library draws cultural sustenance from this triad, offering the reader-researcher the gift of refuge and renewal in a contemplative context. Whether in ancient Alexandria, London in the nineteenth century, or the twenty-first-century networked city, these qualities answer needs keenly felt—and at every point have represented the survival of virtues thought in retreat before the onrushing progress of civilization.[19]

Yet the provision of these goods manifests a contradiction as well. While refuge might seem to be best sought after on mountaintops or in desert wastes, libraries often have presented a cloistering closer to hand—even in the midst of teeming cities. The tension between retreat and connection—between country and city, proximity and alienation, distance and difference, solitude and community—has animated thinking about libraries all along. The digital age further reinforces such

Daily Diary Drop – at the entrance to every local public library there is a drop-off box for patrons who wish to donate diaries and other manuscript materials of minor historical value. The box contains a pouch with small sealable boxes and deposit forms to be filled out by donors. (JS)

tensions. Its neocloisters are the closest of siblings to its living mausolea. If the latter privilege deep storage and retrieval, the former prioritize the leveraging of that deep storage in support of the production of in-depth knowledge. The research community's the thing in a neocloister; the collection remains central but, in the final reckoning, it's a support. Neocloisters are retreats designed to propel advances. They provide a dislocated observational perch in order to ease drilling down beneath the surface of things: into atoms, anatomies, archeological remains, genetic strings, webs of meaning and belief.

In the West, attempts to work out these orders and contrasts galvanized early Christian communities. Cassiodorus, whose long career as a panegyrist and public official spanned some of the most contentious years of the waning Roman world, late in life founded a monastic community on his family estate near the Gulf of Squillace in Calabria.[20] Cassiodorus was active in the sixth century AD, coming to public life in the reign of Theoderic (succeeding the doomed Boethius as *magister* to the Ostrogothic leader). As attested to in the preface to his *Institutiones*, he had sought to found a Christian school in Rome with Pope Agapethus, a Roman equivalent to the School of Alexandria (remembered for such Church Fathers as Clement and Origen), but the venture proved impossible.[21] The Mediterranean world was too riven by quarrels: between the Ostrogoths and Visigoths to the west; between the Italian communities and the increasingly-Romanized Goths in the their midst; between those Goths and the tribes to the north and east, including the Huns; between Goths and the Byzantine seat of power under Justinian in Constantinople; between Arians and Trinitarians in religious discourse. After a long career in Rome, Ravenna, and Constantinople, it was a good time to retreat to monastic living.

As noted earlier, Cassiodorus's community became known as the Vivarium for its fish ponds which, communicating with the Ionian Sea, would have provided a reliable source of sustenance. But the name was also metaphoric, evoking the distinctive charms of monastic life there: a *claustrum* in the literal sense of being a place of enclosure (from the Latin *claudere*), yet flowing with connections to the wider world; placid on the surface, yet teeming with life. A contemporary of Benedict (there is no indication the two monastic leaders ever met), Cassiodorus created a community that sought to hybridize early theories of monastic life, which turned on a dichotomy between the coenobitic, or communitarian, and anchoritic, or hermitic. At the Vivarium, monks could have it both ways: the Vivarium proper was a community, bustling with life and in touch with the wider world; a more remote station called the Castellum, meanwhile, supported the retreat of individual hermits following an ascetic way of life with ties to traditions of the ancient near east.

Straddling the two realities of the Vivarium was its library: a significant library by the standards of the day but, more importantly for purposes of the present argument, a *working* library designed to interconnect practices of reading, prayer, and contemplation. The collection in question was swiftly assembled by Cassiodorus in the course of the community's early years and just as quickly dispersed and lost by the eighth century.[22] It was never envisaged as a library for its own sake. It was understood, rather, as a place of communion between sacred and secular knowledge that would both support and physically express the educational curriculum detailed in the *Institutiones*, which also served as an annotated catalog. Scripture, scriptural exegesis, and commentary provide the foundation. Other works of the Church Fathers follow in close succession, placed in the company of authoritative works of ancient grammar, history, geography, philosophy, literature, and medicine, most of non-Christian deriva-

Empty Shelf Syndrome — as collections migrate off-site, existing stack structures will be reworked as curated exhibition and experience spaces. They will include linear greenhouses, an insectopolis, galleries of unrecognized and unclassified found objects, art installations, and tactile corridors. (IS)

tion. In the cosmos of Cassiodorus, the act of reading is understood as central because indivisible from tasks of writing, speech, annotation, ethical reasoning, prayer, and worship.

On the communitarian side, the Vivarium's ties to the world were not insignificant. Indeed, Cassiodorus's founding of a monastic community was not a turning away from challenging times, but a turning to contemplation and community as necessary ingredients in a modern mix (the historian Lellia Cracco Ruggini points out that *modernus* was a Cassiodoran neologism[23]). While it represented retirement from public life for Cassiodorus, the Vivarium was hardly located in a remote wilderness; indeed, it lay in proximity to trade routes connecting the Ionian Sea with the wider Mediterranean world. Although Squillace remained largely untouched by the destructive energies of the sixth century—the waning hegemony of the Ostrogoths, the victory of Byzantium, and numerous barbarian incursions)—Cassiodorus's Vivarium winked out as a monastic community, while the Rule of St. Benedict flourished throughout Europe.

In the fragile and fraught new world disorder brought about in the wake of the Roman empire's demise, other fortresses of learning and wisdom arose, few more effectively sheltered from the winds of history than the stony redoubt of Mount Athos on the peninsula known to the ancients as Akte, the easternmost blade of the trident of the larger Chalkidike peninsula, which juts into the Aegean from the northern Greek coast. Home to some twenty communities to this day, Athos was a base for monastic activity perhaps as early as the fourth century AD, predating the exertions of Cassiodorus and Benedict. Famously inaccessible, the "holy mountain" preserved a vast trove of codices, relics, and works of Byzantine art. A witness who visited Athos in 1899 attested to the richness, the singularity, and the obscurity of manuscripts treasured up in the libraries there:

> We were much impressed by the number and the beauty
> of the mss. we saw at the Laura. To find that there are
> still more than 200 mss. of the Gospels uncataloged by
> Gregory and uncollated, 120 of them being vellum mss.
> earlier than the fifteenth century, is a surprise, and this
> feeling is increased if it be remembered that there is also a
> similar, though not quite so great a mass of mss. of patristic
> literature [...].[24]

Cultural objects can benefit from their seclusion in the wilderness, especially when under the watchful eye of an entire community of students and researchers. But it's not the only pathway to preservation.

Sometimes, the very ephemerality of things can aid in their preservation, inducing people to attend to them with care. In England, the White Horse of Uffington, an equiform earthwork dating to the late bronze or early iron age, survives to this day even though the grass turf in which it lies embedded, ever-growing, could cover up its chalk figurations in a few short years. Stylized, ropy, big as a soccer pitch, the White Horse seems to fluoresce upon the pastoral green hillside where it rests, in south Oxfordshire's grazing lands. While the White Horse is in the countryside, it's hardly hidden in the wild; it lies about twenty miles southwest of Oxford, not far from the M4, an easy morning's drive from London. Although managed by the National Trust, it survives to this day (and can be plainly seen in Google Earth) chiefly due to a local tradition, "the scouring of the White Horse," in which locals gather every ten years or so to cut back the turf and refresh the chalk. It was described by the author Thomas Hughes in the mid-nineteenth century:

Awesome Box – instead of returning an item to the standard drop-off slot, patrons can promote them via the Awesome Box. All nominated objects are immediately starred in the online catalog. A tweet is issued and they join the family of items included on the Awesome web page where other patrons can view them. (AC, MP)

I should think we must have gone up two hundred steps, when all of a sudden Joe stopped just above me, and called out, "Here we are;" and in about four steps I came to a trench cut into the chalk about two feet deep, which ran up the hill-side right ahead of us. The chalk in the trench was all hard and flat, and seemed to have been scraped and brushed up quite lately. "This is his tail," said Joe. "Come on; look, they're scouring him up above; we're in luck I thought they'd have done before this; and there's the Squire too with 'em." So I looked up; and there, some way above, I saw a lot of men with shovels, and besoms, and barrows, cleaning away at the trench, which, now that I began to look at it, certainly came out more and more like a horse galloping.[25]

It's a favorite object lesson of Stuart Schieber, a computational linguist and director of Harvard's Office of Scholarly Communication, who recommends it as an example for library preservation strategies:

> [T]he survival of the Uffington White Horse is witness
> to a continuous three millennium process of active
> maintenance of this artifact. As such, it provides a perfect
> metaphor for the problems of digital preservation…
> We have no precedent for long-term preservation of
> interpretable digital objects. Unlike books printed on acid-
> free paper, which survive quite well in a context of benign
> neglect, but quite like the White Horse, bits degrade over
> time. It requires a constant process of maintenance and
> repair … to maintain interpretable bits over time scales
> longer than technology-change cycles. By coincidence,
> those time scales are about commensurate with the time
> scales for chalk figure loss, on the order of decades.[26]

We've made a seeming shift: from contemplation to preservation. But if these examples show us anything, it's that one prefigures and frames the other and, in turn, sets us in motion toward the cloister's deeper mission: activation, which is to say research—the proliferation of knowledge itself.

Although he describes laypeople gathering in a festal atmosphere, Schieber's comment also describes the enterprise of monastic attention—which encompasses more than retreat and contemplation, but active practice of the crafts of repair and renewal. The preservative effects of such attention are most evocatively discernible in the survival of the Ise Grand Shrine, a vital Shinto holy site in Japan's Mie prefecture. Not so old as the White Horse, the Ise shrine is venerable, with a history dating to the seventh century AD (and legends stretching back two thousand years).

Ise's main buildings are made of wood, constructed with simple elegance in an architectural style dating to the third century AD. The style perseveres in large part because the shrine is rebuilt every twenty years with cypress wood from a grove cultivated for this purpose. (Last rebuilt in 1993, Ise is undergoing its current renewal at this writing.) What is perhaps most striking about Ise's cycle of rebuilding is that not only have the forms of the buildings been preserved, but a host of ancient carpentry techniques and associated crafts have been handed down through the generations as well. Through its very ephemerality and need for renewal, Ise preserves not only wooden structures, but ways of life as well. Likewise in Benedictine abbeys, Tibetan monasteries, and the sketes of Mount Athos, it was generations of scribal attention—acts of copying undertaken in reverence and contemplative attention—that preserved books and their uses through the centuries.

Many have come to take the liberality of the modern library for granted. This quality is a deep cultural good and yet, when taken for granted, it becomes the ground for mere consumption. In nostalgic takes on the library's role in culture, it's often complained that individuals today lack opportunities for reflection and contemplation. But we too easily forget that these states aren't services offered in some kind of cultural spa, but active efforts to sustain and remake worlds. What would a future library look like if it combined the effervescence of Cassiodorus, the seclusion of Benedict, and the active-contemplative rituals of renewal found at Ise and the Vale of the White Horse?

One could do worse than look to the example of the Clock of the Long Now. In the early 1990s, computer scientist Daniel Hillis noticed that, with the Millennium fast approaching, the "future" seemed to be shrinking year by year: throughout the late twentieth century, the year 2000 remained the mark by which people measured time to come.[27] Wanting to instill a sense of deep time, to awaken an awareness of the long-term consequences of our acts and choices, Hillis imagined a giant mechanical clock—something on the scale of ancient monuments like Stonehenge, the pyramids, and the White Horse—to instill a meditative respect for time and its role in civilization. As an engineer, the construction of a clock intended to run accurately also appealed to Hillis, and he set a heady design goal: to build a mechanism that would function for ten thousand years, a period of time longer than the life of any library, any civilization, any writing system or even language. Securing the participation of a bevy of post-sixties public thinkers including *Wired* founder Kevin Kelly and Stewart Brand of *Whole Earth Catalog* and *The Well* fame, Hillis's clock is slowly but surely becoming a reality: two mountain sites, in Nevada and Texas, are now in building phases. Each will host giant, elegantly-engineered clocks, built with technology that marries the bronze age to the computer era, designed to measure the passage of years, days, and hours, as well as the movements of astronomical bodies.

Ruletimes – instead of operating under a single set of rules, the library adopts variable rules. During the school day, the reading room operates as a social space with a noise level appropriate for conversation; in the afternoon it becomes a study room under a blanket of silence; at night it becomes a place of noisy literate recreation. (JS)

The movements of these monumental timepieces will depend in part on the active participation of people—pilgrims, perhaps, moved by secular reverence for time—to keep them wound. And each will contain an affordance that has been part of Hillis's vision from the beginning: a library.

The Long Now Clock is an astonishing vision—so astonishing that it's easy to forget how many of its qualities already appear in extant institutions. After all, the Cloister was always a place entrusted with timekeeping of the deepest sort. In the era of Benedict, it kept liturgical time on the basis of heavenly movements whose every tick marked the progress of salvation history; in the modern era, it provides the time of contemplation required for the production and reproduction of knowledge. The cloister works its magic as a working library, a haven of books and study, where adepts set themselves apart for a time to commune in intellectual labor. At institutes such as the Salk, the Getty, and the Santa Fe, as on many a sequestered campus environment, intellectual work is pursued in cloistered cultivation. Such places offer their arguments toward seclusion architecturally and situationally: the shifting, subtle colorations of the Santa Fe Institute's desert locale offer a piquant contrast to the foment of its scientific community; the Getty's resident scholars grapple with the ethereal and the aesthetic on a mountaintop aerie overlooking the vibrantly mundane city of Los Angeles; at the Salk, Louis Kahn's procession of tiered and louvered concrete buildings act as a concentration engine, framing a life-sustaining Pacific whose fecundity and fragility inspire the biologists who work within. Likewise, campus architectures from Oxbridge to liberal arts colleges such as Bryn Mawr and Reed, often modeled explicitly upon medieval monasteries, feature a working library—not a storehouse for books but a workplace for students and teachers that serves as the focal point of community and residential life.[28] "This is their laboratory," writes Charles Rufus Morey, Princeton art history professor and creator of the influential cataloged repertory of photographs known as the Index of Christian Art, "quite as important an element in the working life of these departments as any laboratory is to that of a scientific department [...] It is just as essential that the undergraduates, graduate students, and staff of each of these departments be placed in the closest and most convenient contact with their books and with each other, as it is that a research worker in science should be within the easy reach of his apparatus."[29] The library as laboratory, the laboratory as library; the library lab, the labrary: there's a dreamed-of meshing of knowledge spaces here that may be distinctive to the modern era but has deep historical roots.

And while these cloisters have their libraries, there are also latter-day libraries that host their own cloisters: think of the Cullman Center at the New York Public Library, offering writers and scholars a year of seclusion in the midst of a city that never sleeps. In distinction from the Long Now Clock's focus on Deep Time, in these places, Deep Knowledge is the quality to be celebrated and won.

Deep Time is a secular instantiation of the divine power, encompassing both enormity and the sublime, which the cloisters sought not to escape, but to ponder. What took the form of wheels of fire and world-consuming floods for the ancients now fixes the attention in varied forms: at Getty, the elusive flicker of beauty and its history; at Santa Fe and the Salk, biogenesis, cosmology, and the threat of climate change. In the dazzle of data the world offers us, we can produce a torrent of books, an information tsunami—or we can go together into seclusion and parse the stream. Thus in the cloister do the two qualities, Deep Time and Deep Knowledge, come to stand in transitive relation, with the latter standing as the human operating upon the former.

Stack U – flexible wired classrooms are carved out of existing stack structures becoming hubs for the delivery of Massive Open Online Courses with on-site instructors. The walls of the enclosures become staging grounds for bibliography and support materials for the ongoing MOOCs. (JS)

W. A. Renwick standing in front of nearly complete Electronic Delay Storage Automatic Calculator (EDSAC) at the University of Cambridge Mathematical Laboratory (early 1949). © Computer Laboratory, University of Cambridge.

Database

An ocean of words; a torrent of books; a library of Babel: they're necessary, these imaginings of knowledge run amok. The author of the last, that laureate of the library, Jorge Luis Borges, also imagined a map that tries to take over the world:

> …In that empire, the art of cartography attained such perfection that the map of a single province occupied the entirety of a city, and the map of the empire, the entirety of a province. In time, those unconscionable maps no longer satisfied, and the cartographers' guilds struck a map of the empire whose size was that of the empire, and which coincided point for point with it. The following generations, who were not so fond of the study of cartography as their forebears had been, saw that that vast map was useless, and not without some pitilessness was it, that they delivered it up to the inclemencies of sun and winters. In the deserts of the west, still today, there are tattered ruins of that map, inhabited by animals

and beggars; in all the land there is no other relic of the
disciplines of geography.[30]

Looking at Google Earth—not only with its global coverage,
but with its feral knittings-together of night and day, summer
and winter, the view from the street and God's-eye view; its
uncanny, algorithmic transpositions and elisions—we might
be tempted to say that Borges's Ozymandian cartographers
have struck again. It's important to remember, however, that
Google Earth is the instantiation of a database: a different
knowledge-object and symbolic form from the map, though
hardly unrelated. Indeed it's a database through and through.
The base map consists of "tiles" of imagery with metadata
telling the software to stitch *this* tile to *this* tile and *these* to
these in cascading orders of magnitude; layers of cartographic information—names of rivers and mountains, monuments
and transit stations, national borders and private businesses,
even the photographs uploaded and shared by world travel-
ers. All of these exist as data in databases, programmatically
linked to and expressed upon the map. To say "upon," however, is already to submit to the cartographic fiction that the
map represents a territory, a surface, upon which figurations
are inscribed. With maps, it's data—chosen, organized, and
massaged—all the way down.

In the thirteenth century Mediterranean world, mari-
ners developed a way of mapping that reduced the world to
data—perhaps we should say *wove a world from data*—in a
peculiarly effective way. Portolan charts, which paid rigorous
attention to coastlines, organized locations according to
compass headings.[31] The chartmakers made their maps according to the spatial logic of the compass, then situated
ports, coves, and harbors within that logic. In so doing, *portolani* changed the nature of the information pilots had long

relied upon. Previously, this information was controlled through storytelling: in their periplus books, navigators had long organized such information in narrative form; now they could supplement those storified accounts with another tool, one that spatialized the data in useful, complementary ways.

The database, like the *portolani* to which it is tied, has its characteristic cultural effects. These derive from its peculiar materiality, its embodiedness in digital computation, which from the start was organized along the axis of noun and verb. As Lev Manovich describes it,

> Computer programming encapsulates the world according to its own logic. The world is reduced to two kinds of software objects which are complementary to each other: data structures and algorithms. Any process or task is reduced to an algorithm, a final sequence of simple operations which a computer can execute to accomplish a given task. And any object in the world — be it the population of a city, or the weather over the course of a century, a chair, a human brain — is modeled as a data structure, i.e. data organized in a particular way for efficient search and retrieval[...] Together, data structures and algorithms are two halves of the ontology of the world according to a computer.[32]

"The world according to the computer"—only is it a world, or the tattered ruin of its map?

Manovich further observes that we're inclined to view data as passive and algorithm as active: "another example of passive-active binary categories so loved by human cultures."[33] In this way, a database seems to fulfill certain expectations we have of the libraries we know so well. Indeed, there are crucial ways in which libraries do seem databases:

Poster Post-Its — as patron activity shifts to online environments, it loses its visibility. In order to reestablish this visibility, the main data sets that represent a day's activity are automatically translated into poster-sized color maps printed out every day and placed in a gallery that tracks the past ten days in the library's life. (JS, JY)

they are hierarchically organized arrays of information, after all, responsive to search and retrieval behaviors.

But there are differences. First, digital data are computationally accessible and relatable in ways text had never reduced to before; every object made from data has the capacity to be a database itself. Thus in the digital library, books are not only data points in a catalog; they are also databases unto themselves, nested within databases, with links to outside databases in which they are data points as well. The web itself is, in important ways, no more than a giant database. "Borges's story about a map which was equal in size to the territory it represented became re-written as the story about databases and the data they index," Manovich observes. "But now the map has become larger than the territory."

The opportunities, as well as the pitfalls, of massed data are nothing new; they're part of the modern condition. Elizabeth Eisenstein was one of the first and most effective at limning the revolutionary effects of massed data.[34] In her account, the Rudolphine Tables of Johannes Kepler are not a foundational achievement because they contained extraordinarily accurate measurements of the movements of heavenly bodies, although that they did. Rather, their contribution comes in the form of their very materiality: having been printed, they could be accessed and consulted by a widespread community of thinkers and observers, now freed from the burden of copying them out.[35] Not only could such readers consult Kepler's figures; they now had access to multiple tables and other sources of information, ancient and modern; rather than slavishly accepting the authority of a given *auctor* represented by a small number of manuscripts, thinkers could now amass information, comparing it forensically, judging it analytically, combining it synthetically.

Yet there were costs associated with such richness. As historian Ann Blair notes, "the authors of [early modern] reference books presented themselves as compilers, responsible for the accurate reporting of what others had written elsewhere but not for the veracity of those statements themselves".[36] Blair discusses how thinkers had begun to suspect that the compilation of information had gotten out of hand. "Even if all knowledge could be found in books, where it is already mixed in with so many useless things and confusingly heaped in such large volumes," wrote Descartes, "it would take longer to read those books than we have to live in this life."[37] Indeed, Descartes's skeptical embrace of accumulated knowledge in achieving understanding is one of the qualities that makes him modern. And yet these issues were hardly new. The ancients, too, had worried about the nonsense treasured up in books, and the faulty tools of memory and cogitation we humans must use to sort the gold from the dross. Among them, Seneca famously compared the restless reader to a person who travels widely but forges no lasting friendships. "The same must needs be the case with people who never set about acquiring an intimate acquaintanceship with any one great writer," he muses, "but skip from one to another, paying flying visits to them all. [...] A multitude of books only gets in one's way."[38]

These were some of the responses to the challenges of information overload in the form of books, which built on the challenges with information overload that had already been experienced with codices, scrolls, and memorized data. At the same time that the printing press was revolutionizing the kinds and sheer amount of information available to readers in book form, the *portolani* were being used to extend the knowledge-gathering net to new hemispheres in the early-modern burst of voyaging and discovery. With new kinds of knowledge came new acts of oppression and expropriation. It's perhaps a bit of a stretch to say that colonial depredations were effects of knowledge overload, but only slightly so.

By slow degrees, early modern libraries became a crucial part of the effort to manage knowledge amid a torrent of print. Medieval libraries sought to tend the flame of knowledge, to keep the glowing ember from going out altogether; they operated within a media ecology where scarcity was the norm, so the conservation of even trivial or fragmentary forms of textual data, especially from the distant past, was second nature. Now the project became one of keeping an inferno in check. Libraries were no longer sites of copying, but of comparing; no longer of compiling but of cataloging, collating, and no small amount of comparing, cutting, and controlling. Libraries and archives became sites of new disciplinary techniques for knowledge.

As Edward Hutchins has shown, maps and other information tools are never self-sufficient embodiments of information; they're everywhere caught up in crafts, techniques, practices, and social arrangements that articulate their qualities and body forth the knowledge they make available in acts of shared cognition.[39] Following Manovich and Alan Liu, we can see how the database too gives rise to its own set of cultural practices and aesthetic norms; many of these are remixes of prior moves, while some are *sui generis*. Crucially—and this too is a Borgesian proposition—the database creates its own retrospective genealogy, infecting prior forms and causing them to appear uncannily database-like in some of their effects. A story, for example, now seems less like a natural account of a chain of cause and effect than an instantiation of a search operation carried out across in-world events, a choosing of plausible connections from a database of actions. The story, in other words, begins to seem like an interface. Acts in the world, by the same token, are no longer ephemeral phenomena or sense-impressions of ideal forms, but data susceptible to organizing, linking, and algorithmic transfor-

Labrary II – the library becomes a site for research on learning tools, with patrons volunteering to give up their privacy and serve as test subjects, much as volunteers do in medical trials. Offline vs. online behaviors are studied, as are differing patterns of consultation and reading between analog and digital supports. (JK)

mation. Increasingly, our every act becomes reducible to tabular data, to collation, and control beyond our comprehension.

How can libraries help to mediate the practical, aesthetic, and ethical challenges of living in a world of databases? They can start responding to information overload in the database age not only by *being* databases, but by helping users to interpret and understand them as well. David Weinberger:

> A library platform will give access not only to all of the
> content it has access to directly and indirectly — the items
> on its shelves, the e-items it has permission to provide,
> and the items (physical and virtual) within its network
> of collaborating institutions — but also to all the data it
> can find: Data from a curated set of reliable institutions,
> including scientific and non-profit. Data from the local
> government, and from all levels of government. Content
> contributed by local members, such as digitized shoeboxes
> of local scenes. Some of this data may be available elsewhere,
> but the library can provide the service of making this data
> more usable by aggregating it (or pointers to it), certifying it
> as reliable and interesting, cataloging it, documenting it, and
> helping users to navigate it and understand it.[40]

We treat data as fungible, as platform-independent, and yet everywhere we find it transformed by the material means of its capture and analysis. We talk about raw data, and yet it is everywhere already cooked. Librarians long struggled with the challenges of bringing books to heel, tempering quantity and quality, the exoteric and the esoteric, access and control. In the late twentieth century, they did this in large part through the application of databases: controlling, massaging, storing, and sharing information about books. But rarely have libraries seen data—even their own collections data, much less other kinds of datasets—as cultural objects, as texts of a kind, susceptible to curation, interpretation, and sharing with library publics. We've mastered the (largely metaphorical) operation of the library as a database; now, it's time to become a library of databases. It's all too easy to lose track of the territory of the world amid the tattered maps of data we produce. All the more reason for librarians to become data navigators, charting their practical *portolani* for passengers in the information storms of the internet age.

We're seeing the emergence of such institutions, which operationalize the database not as guide to or control over the library, but as library *tout court*. The Digital Public Library of America, for instance, is a database not in metaphor but in actual fact: at its heart, it is a linked collection of information about allied collections of cultural-heritage resources (metadata, in information-science parlance). This still-young initiative, which was incubated at the Berkman Center for Internet and Society and now exists as an independent nonprofit institution, is quickly gathering a collection of collections from such partners as the Smithsonian, the Biodiversity Heritage Library, and the HathiTrust, as well as many state and local archival collections. As the DPLA grows, its patrons will make use of increasingly diverse kinds of collections through an interface conceived not as a portal, but a platform: not as a way to view pieces of collections, but to put them into dialogue with one another; not as mere source of information, but as a user-centered location that lives and thrives thanks to the extraordinary range of things that users do with and to collections.

To effect this kind of interactivity, the DPLA is following the example of other national heritage digitization efforts like Europeana[41] and the National Library of Australia's Trove,[42] offering users access to an API, or application programming interface. An API is like a digital pipe fitting, allowing code-savvy users[43] to create their own programs that access, analyze, and transform these collections databases dynamically. While a traditional online library catalog lets users search by author, title, or keyword and see lists of records that match the search term, an API makes it possible to tell stories about the history, nature, and social life of collections: visualizations that express a library's interest in foreign-language titles over time, for instance, or mappings of the publication of an author's work by edition to gauge the spread of her influence through communities and around the world.

Such toolkits will enrich future libraries and beyond-the-book collections, to be sure. But they're possible now, even in our oldest, richest, most conservative libraries, which already exist in database form. One of our curatorial innovation fellows at metaLAB, Travis Bost, became interested in the landscape paintings of nonsense poet Edward Lear, the largest collection of which is held in Houghton Library's Department of Printing and Graphic Arts. Through a special arrangement, we were able to gain access to the underlying metadata for the collection's 3500 paintings (which existed in a file encoded in a version of XML, to be specific). With these data in hand, Travis wrote a computer program to identify every location, every paint color, every kind of paper in the collection, organizing them all into an elegant visualization that told stories about Lear's career as a landscape artist that could not be discerned from a textual listing of the collection itself. None of this required the collection of new data or the redescription of works in the repository; all of it was possible based on the careful work of description undertaken by archivists of prior generations. As David Weinberger observes, "libraries know a lot more than the combined content of the items in their collection. They know what librarians know. They know what catalogers know. They know what their users know. And they know a huge amount about the social life of their works."[44] The missing link: a user-centered interface that expresses a collection's full potential as a database, that turns the library catalog from a portal into a platform—perhaps starting with a simple button in the browser that says, give me the data now and let me do (creative) things with it.

There can be little question that databases are one of the defining library types of the present era or that their role in the future of knowledge forms will continue to dilate in importance. But, like every one of our other types, they possess powers as well as limits. Potentially available everywhere where networks are present, their ties to physical world remain fluid and fungible. After all, what kind of *place* is a database (even a database like Google Earth)? Is a database a place at all? Given that a majority of the world's knowledge is location-based, given the key role that space and place play in every human culture and society, a library endowed exclusively with an infinitely portable, virtual architectonics, no matter how replete and complete and user-friendly, may prove lacking and incomplete from a socio-cultural standpoint. In the absence of a physical plant, how can a DPLA or Europeana, for instance, fulfill not just the mission of conjoining collections on a massive scale, but also build a sense of shared community or link local realities and resources to the global mainstream? All the more so given that the interactions and identities forged within even the best designed user-centric database environments tend to pale in comparison with the significance of those forged face-to-face. How might bridges be built between existing physical infrastructures, like those provided in the form of brick-and-mortar civic spaces by public library systems, and our glowing global databases?

An Amazon distribution warehouse employing the so-called "chaotic storage" method of organization. Such warehouse facilities can attain sizes of up to 1.2 million square feet. Photograph by SippingTea, November 2009; CC license 2.0.

Accumulibrary

Whereas the living mausoleum and the cloister have many centuries of history and databases are at least fifty years old, the Accumulibrary is an institutional fiction as of yet untested and untried, but plausible. It instantiates the database in the physical world.

The Accumulibrary is both dumb and smart: "dumb" because based on the willy-nilly heaping together of resources—so-called "chaotic storage"; "smart" because built around the capabilities of an omniscient database that monitors locations and items within its otherwise mobile confines and renders them at once intelligible and accessible. The notion of a place of warehousing or temporary holding for large corpora of manuscripts, documents, scrolls, or books has historical precedents in various epochs though, strictly speaking, none were understood as "libraries." One thinks of the great waterfront storehouses of ancient Alexandria, thought by some to have been at the origin of the great fire that went on to destroy the library itself; or of the *genizoth*, places of hiding lo-

Premium Options – instead of a single-tiered service model, libraries adopt a multi-tiered approach. Baseline levels of service are guaranteed to all. But for citizens who pursue data-intensive lives or whose work requires special access, fee-based programs provide higher levels of support and personalized research assistance. (JK)

cated in synagogues or Jewish cemeteries where materials were parked, sometimes for centuries, awaiting the proper burial required by Talmudic law. (The most celebrated is the Cairo Geniza with its over 280,000 manuscript fragments, composed between 860 AD and the nineteenth century.) Similarly, but now with an overtly commercial ethos animating their labors and the beginnings of a database backbone, early booksellers like Luc'antonio and Filippo Giunti (Venice), Giovanni Bartolomeo da Gabiano (Venice, Lyon), Giovanni Varisco (Venice), and Giovanni Giolito (Turin) built networks of stockage facilities, supported by inventorying and book-keeping systems that were state-of-the-art by Renaissance standards.[45]

The Accumulibrary is the indirect descendant of such bookseller warehouses. But it draws its direct inspiration from contemporary big box stores and the distribution warehouses of firms like Amazon.com. It weds the frugal interiors of the big-box store with the randomly organized megawarehouse in the service of a flexible, expansive, democratized concept of the research library.

The Accumulibrary rejects taxonomy as a founding principle. It shuns all local and universal schemes of organization and is indifferent as regards the virtues of spatial economy, temporal sequence, and alphabetic order. Its exterior is box-like and modular. Its interior is characterized by a lack of subdivisions, naked concrete slab floors, high ceilings (with readily visible overhead storage space), and horizontal sprawl (the whole is visible from any elevated perch). Its furnishings are practical. Robust, adjustable, and moveable, they shun all decorative touches and the warmth of wood, not to mention gestures toward permanence or recognition of the importance of creature comforts. Thanks to its modular low-cost construction techniques and standardized shelving systems, space is abundant and additional capacity always potentially available. In the Accumulibrary, the freedom to accumulate ever more things is in lockstep with the freedom to add on ever more space.

Unlike modern libraries, the Accumulibrary doesn't segment or segregate media types. It fails to differentiate documents from things, books from periodicals from pamphlets, devices from objects, the new from the used from the old, the rare from the common. The sole laws that it holds sacred are the law of number and the law of stuff. The *law of number* because every item and every location within the Accumulibrary's matrix of shelving lanes is tagged with barcodes devised not for human browsers but for the sensory organs and memories of machines. The *law of stuff* because materials are organized not by author, title, theme, subject matter, language, or discipline, but as a function of their order of arrival and the practical imperatives of location and relocation. Whenever and wherever a gap opens up in the storage system, it is randomly filled. Everything in an Accumulibrary is on the move.

Serendipitous discovery remains as much a possibility within this titanic ark of documents, devices, and things as it does within the programmable library. But it assumes a singular character. Discovery is jarring and disjunctive, like the Count of Lautréamont's "encounter of a sewing machine with an umbrella on a dissection table."[46] Browsing the stacks of the Accumulibrary is thus less akin to drifting down the curated corridors of a warburghian *Denkraum* (see the next section) in pursuit of an epiphany than to surveying the motley stalls of a sprawling flea market. The cognitive strain is overwhelming. There's much too much to take in. It's a world made up of differences without transitions. Perhaps it's the positive double of Borges's "subaltern horror": the Total Library—"the vast, contradictory Library, whose vertical wildernesses of books run the incessant risk of changing into others that affirm, deny, and confuse everything like a delirious god."[47]

Chaos is congenial to the Accumulibrary: the sort of hypercontrolled chaos embodied by Amazon's distribution warehouses. In the latter, incoming goods are ferried directly from the landing dock to unoccupied slots within a universal shelving system irrespective of their size or character. Every location and item is barcoded. Handheld scanners relay the barcoded data to a central database that monitors inventories, maintains a real-time map of the warehouse floor, and generates efficient picking lists for the purpose of fulfilling orders. The layout of the shelving lanes is flexible and can be quickly remapped as a function of changing storage or retrieval needs or anticipated shifts in supply and demand.

The Accumulibrary adopts a similar approach, though its pickers are reader-patrons fulfilling personal research orders. Before entering the warehouse proper, they settle into a booth in the Command Center where, working with a reference accumulibrarian, they jointly devise what is referred to as a "knowledge walk" and are equipped with a hand-held scanner and a floor plan. A "knowledge walk" is a printout with an algorithmically generated itinerary accompanied by a map based on a set of search terms and queries. It consists in a curated pathway amidst the shelving for the purpose of retrieving and consulting objects and works, exploring ideas, familiarizing oneself with a given era or field, or engaging in cultural-historical treasure hunts. It can be programmed to fall anywhere on the spectrum between a maximally efficient path to a pathway informed by maximal drift. Pathways may also be devised to fulfill non-research-centered objectives: like tracing an ideal geometry, game playing, or maximizing aerobic benefits.

Some of the artifacts within the Accumulibrary are circulating. Others are not. In the case of circulating objects, the patron simply scans the barcode on his library smart card, the object and location barcodes, and pops it in his cart. Non-circulating items may be checked out locally and examined in the study islands located in every quadrant of the warehouse. A sensor system impedes their removal from the quadrant in question, but they can be photographed, scanned, and verbally annotated with the assistance of a hand-held scanner. The resulting files are automatically uploaded via the local wifi network onto servers and saved in a personalized online folder. Once an object has been removed from its prior location, that location is filled with a new, freshly arrived object. Upon a borrowed item's return, it migrates to the nearest existing gap and is reentered in the central database.

Locations within the Accumulibrary are always known. But they are never permanent due to circulation flows, shifting usage patterns and patron demands, accessioning and deaccessioning ebbs and flows, and the arrival or transfer of entire collections. Movement is both lateral and vertical, with less utilized materials tending to gradually drift upward into the less immediately accessible overhead storage areas and more utilized materials gravitating downward toward the floor level. Barcoding and re-barcoding are constants, so the same knowledge walk is likely to entail a significantly different path from one month to the next. The intelligibility and navigability of the Accumulibrary's space depends entirely upon information systems. When these go down, it becomes a data wilderness and junkyard, a disorderly dumping ground where patrons and librarians alike can do little more than scavenge on the basis of outdated recollections and pray for lucky finds.

For all the no-frills austerity of the warehouse itself, the Accumulibrary remains a place that is welcoming to patrons. But only in the glass-enclosed balcony that runs around the building's periphery known as the Skydeck. The Skydeck allows visitors to settle down in a club-like environment and to study materials and collections, whether individually or in groups, while gazing out upon the spectacle of the main floor. Instead of providing a conventional reading room experience, it is programmed to accommodate varying noise and distraction levels, music and video, even food and drink. A portion of one wing serves as an audiovisual production studio, fabrication lab, and maker space, complete with a "library" of professional editing, animation, and modeling work stations. Another area houses a writer- and artist-in-residence program, a performance space, and a book art workshop. Yet another serves as a hacker space where patrons are encouraged to slice and dice the Accumulibrary's data sets and to print out their visualizations of collections flows, circulation data, and past and present patron knowledge walks on wall sized plotters, thereby adding ever new strata to the hacker space's Viz Wall. In one of the Skydeck's corners, there exists a small gallery space, known as The Shrine, that documents the most memorable, imaginative, and eccentric knowledge walks that have been performed in the history of the Accumulibrary.

Scannebago Brigades – a swarm of mobile scanning units branches out across the continent, speed-scanning local collections and archives, and assembling them into databases. Initial rough sorting and tagging is carried out online by the donating institutions in collaboration with interested researchers and the public. (JP)

Oval reading room at the Kulturwissenschaftliche Bibliothek Warburg in Hamburg with curated panels, shelves, projector, and epidiascope (1926). Source: Warburg Institute, London.

Universal Programmable Library

If the Accumulibrary is a disorderly warehouse-like hypothetical descendant of the traditional library, the Universal Programmable Library is an orderly double that conjures up a flexible physical architecture aimed at promoting combinatory thinking and serendipitous discovery.

We've argued elsewhere that a library might be a model *for* the world, or a model *of* it. There is the canonical library, which collects the good, the beautiful, and the true, which expresses the ideal, which dreams the world as it should be; and the universal research collection, which strives to document the world's knowledge as quickly as it is produced, privileging documentary quality and comprehensiveness over aesthetic or intellectual or moral concerns (operating with a set of normative qualms, to be sure). But there exists an intermediary prospect. Between the library as polemic on one hand and portrait on the other, we can imagine a matrix for projective reconfigurations of ideas, stories, and information. The Programmable Library is such a library. It is a propositional machine that configures instead of just collecting. Amenable to the whims of individual or collective thinking, speculative probing or perceived need, generative in character, a countermeasure to what Walter Benjamin refers to as "the mild boredom of order," it conforms to criteria that are exploratory rather than definitive, playful rather than predictable.[48] The programmable library delivers provisional lines of inquiry and lanes of action that can provide the basis for future acts of reprogramming.

However peaceable it may seem, the library remains a scene of ceaseless struggle between epistemology and the material: here, intellectual repletion and physical constraint meet in suspension, like oil and water bubble and pool without intermingling. The paradigmatic apprehension of the contents of the thoroughly-cataloged library is computationally trivial. And yet in its granularity and scale, the book stack resists immediate human comprehension. The computer, by contrast, loses purchase precisely where we humans excel: in the perception of pattern amid noise, in the identification of the camouflaged figure against cluttered ground, in the oblique sorting and sifting of titles hovering at threshold of an information seeker's peripheral vision. Browsing the library—seeking not only sense but inspiration in the flux—is not only a joy; it's also an efficient Turing Test, sorting the human qualities from the machinic.

It was Horace Walpole who put the word "serendipity" into circulation; his coinage was inspired by a Persian tale about three princes "who were always making discoveries, by accident or sagacity, of things they were not in quest of."[49] Longstanding modes of scholarly and contemplative activity have evolved to incorporate serendipitous drift as method— as an exploratory mode quite different from, indeed opposed to, notions of fortune. Where luck is necessarily random but fickle and capricious in the bestowal, serendipity relies on the sagacity Walpole mentions, a "prepared mind," in Pasteur's

Neogymnasia – libraries are built that revive the ancient ideal of the gymnasion (γυμνάσιον) as a place of physical, intellectual, and social exertion. Neogymnasia combine a gym with places of conversation and study and lecture halls. Staffed by trainer-librarians-public health workers, it provides counseling and testing. (JS, MB)

famous formulation, being the prerequisite of the fortunate discoverer. It is in science, indeed, where serendipity is transformed into a methodologically-normative principle, shaping research in ways that permit the identification and isolation of surprising results. For all its seeming method, its certitude, its algorithmic systematicity, science as it emerged in western culture consists in a series of practical operations designed to produce and frame anomaly—in its very precision, a kind of scapulimancy of surprise.

Discovery by means of considered acts of aleatory reading and scanning have a rich history extending back to the beginnings of written records. They were famously formalized in ancient practices of divination, from the performance and interpretation of oracles to the *sortes homericae* and *virgilianae*: forms of bibliomancy in which randomly selected passages of an epic poem were granted predictive or advisory value. The most celebrated such episode in the history of Western culture is the scene of Augustine of Hippo's conversion in book eight of his *Confessions* where, in the midst of a profound spiritual crisis, shedding a river of tears beneath a fig tree, he hears the call of a childlike voice to "pick up and read" (*tolle, lege*). The former rhetor rises up, walks over to grasp his copy of Paul's Epistle to the Romans, where the passage he opens to (Romans 13:13-15) provides a definitive gloss on his entire life. The effect is instantaneous: "I neither wished nor needed to read further. At once, with the last words of this sentence, it was as if a light of relief from all anxiety flooded into my heart. All the shadows of doubt were dispelled." In addition to requiring a state of acute receptivity, the success of such operations is dependent upon the choice of an authoritative text, corpus, or collection from which to draw. The very gesture of random selection is structured, informed by example and precedent: in the case of Augustine, of Anthony the Great's conversion to the ascetic life through the discovery of Matthew 19:21. Planned accidents find a congenial home within the confines of a bound volume, a curated bookshelf, or the labyrinth of a programmed library.

The stack itself offers seemingly limitless opportunities for the prepared mind to find conjunctions and synchronicities or to wander productively. And yet those possible conjunctions among the books, however vast in number, are limited—not only by the size of the collection (as Borges's great short story "Library of Babel" reminds us), but by the catalog, by whatever ordering principle determines which books stand next to one another on the shelves.[50] If we think of a library as a kind of machine—an engine for learning, provocation, and discovery—it can take us many places. Following the metaphor to its end, however, we realize that this bibliomantic machine might have a speed limit, its governor taking the form of the fixed set of locatively-possible permutations. A question suggests itself: how might we design a more nimble and productive mechanism of serendipity into the physical makeup of the library? What if the classification system were no longer fixed but flexible; if the books returned not to accustomed places on the shelves, but to entirely new locations; if the machine were metamorphic: today, a limo; tomorrow, a sports car; next year, a sedan, perhaps in keeping with the evolving needs of an entire society?

The prospect is not unprecedented and, to varying degrees and on varying time-scales, informs early- to mid-twentieth century debates on the redesign of traditional libraries. For the architect and shelving system designer Angus Snead Macdonald, the key issue was to reject the rigid monumentalism (not to mention, elitism) of inherited library architectures in favor of a modular approach, based on elasticity, interchangeability, and adaptability, that would minimize the interference provided by a building's structure. Only 25% of a library need be dedicated to static functions. The rest could be:

> dynamic and unique [...] there are no fixed locations in
> this major portion—not even as to the walls. The walls are
> made of unit panels insulated against heat transmission
> and interlocking with window sections and with deck
> floors in such a way that they may be taken down and
> reassembled in a new location. In this way we have made
> an expansible building that may be enlarged peripherally
> (but also vertically), by adding new layers of our 'inter-
> changeable' general utility space as required. These layers
> are analogous to the annual rings of a tree trunk except
> that our rings will be spaced at intervals of a decade.[51]

An automatic electric information board guides patrons
through the living, growing organism that is a library built upon
individualism and the pursuit of personal interests (not regi-
mentation), but whose very form dynamically mirrors a community's evolving needs.

One of the liveliest and most fascinating research libraries
is the one amassed by art historian Aby Warburg, who conceived
of his library not as a passive collection, but as a *Denkinstru-
ment*—a flexible, manipulable tool for prying out fresh ideas.
Warburg organized his classification scheme according to a the-
matized "law of good neighborliness," as Christopher Johnson
points out in his recent study of Warburg's comparative and clas-
sificatory methods.[52] Warburg laid out his library according to a
fourfold scheme, devoting a floor to the categories "image,"
"word," "orientation," and "action"—which, to Warburg's way of
thinking, reflected a kind of ontogeny of cultural development,
from visual perception to language to religious belief to politics.
(The Warburg Library in London follows this scheme today.) As
Johnson tells it, "Warburg frequently undertook the reordering
of parts of the Library's collection [...] a few months before his
death, increasingly convinced of (Giordano) Bruno's central

place in early modern intellectual history, Warburg proposed another *Umstellung* (reordering) [...] [A] library, Warburg believed, *ideally works to disrupt conventional classifications of ideas or things in order to produce novel thoughts.*" [53]

There is something in Warburg's restless restructuring of the *Denkraum* that exceeds the rhizomatic. His is not the library as inflorescence, as branching network, nor as many-to-many rootstock, but as a *murmuration*—the fifteenth-century poet John Lydgate's evocative word for a flock of starlings, whose reckless flow encodes a hidden order at once algorithmic and improvisatory. The murmur of the library and the flocking of books, pages fluttering and flying, scattering and recombining, the reader setting a trap like the *vogelval* in Bruegel's *Winter Landscape*—Warburg might agree that when it comes to imagining future libraries, there is iconicity to conjure with here that transports us from mere networks to the strategically laid, crafted bird-trappers net.

It goes without saying that the stack need not be static. Systems of so-called mobile or compact storage, in use in libraries, museums, and archives at least since the 1880s, have evolved dramatically over the past century. [54] After the revolving bookcases and book trucks of the Victorian era came the sliding, suspended, and hinging bookcases of the early twentieth century, and by the century's second half, small-scale, crank-actuated, rolling shelf units. In their aftermath, libraries now make use of automated compact storage on the scale of cargo containers. Whole stacks now exist in the form of sleek steel modules nestled together as tightly as so many shelved volumes, gliding apart on tracks at the touch of a button to reveal aisles of browseable books. To cite one local example, the ranks of compact shelving found in Harvard's Pusey Library, the sepulchrally-fluorescent, compactly-shelved underground bookstack attached to Widener via a series of steam pipe-lined underground tunnels, breed dark fantasies of the shelves sliding shut again to crush lost and lonely readers between the books; in fact, the systems are perfectly safe, with pressure-sensing plates in the floors that disable the drive mechanism. But for the silence and frequent solitude, Pusey's shelving system feels a bit like a kind of ideal mass-transit system: the reader waits while the ranges soundlessly part, then steps slightly up onto the gently-tilting pressure plates, as if boarding a slowgoing ferry full of books. The crossing is always smooth. The walls of books recompress in the traveler's immediate wake.

Movable compact shelving is not the only system for maximizing space in the stack. At the Harvard Depository, which we explore in the visual/verbal coda to this book, volumes are barcoded and boxed as a function of their size, the boxes put up in shelving units fifty feet high and hundreds of feet deep, the books retrieved by staff driving and attached to cranes, who navigate following waypoints determined by computer. A kindred system, known as ASRS (for automated storage retrieval system), long in use in the automobile industry, has been deployed in the underground stack of the Mansueto Library at the University of Chicago. Next to the Regenstein Library, the Brutalist reinforced concrete, limestone-faced ziggurat that has served as Chicago's main library since 1970, the Mansueto lies crouched and cool, a low lozenge of steel-laced glass. At only 58,700 square feet, it's a stealthy campus presence when compared with its predecessor (Regenstein encloses fully 577,085 square feet). That's because, beneath the domed reading room, the stack drops down six floors into the earth, a subterranean book-mine holding up to 3.5 million volumes where 50-foot tall walls of shelves are prowled by robotic cranes that automatically deliver trunkloads of books, per reader request, to the sun-splashed library above.[55] Mansueto's stack turns the physical library into a programmatically-accessible database; the system that directs the robotic book-miners could be recoded along Warburgian lines to deliver remixed serendipity by the boxful or to layer the entire collection according to color, size, date of publication or the first names of donors, printers, binders or borrowers.

Now for the speculative turn: imagine the programmable book stack not as a remote, industrialized warehouse, but as a magical space, where bookshelves dance and weave at the librarians' behest—where, at the launch of a search query, the books swiftly flock and congregate in novel patterns, where books endowed with memories and a network identity inch closer and closer to other books on the basis of the online reading habits of a research community, forming an ever shifting spatial sodality.

Technically, this fairytale scene no longer presents an unsolvable technical problem: in automated order-fulfillment systems used by online retailers, warehouses are equipped with ranks of shelving units that ride on the backs of swift-moving robots, who deliver whole shelves of inventoried product to the hands of shipping staff. Following networks of barcodes on the warehouse floor, the go-cart-sized robots tunnel under ranks of shelves until the called-for unit is found, whereupon they screw themselves to a gimbal underneath, lift the shelving unit, and trundle off to shipping personnel at the periphery of the system. Already, books are being managed in this way; in May 2012, Amazon bought Kiva Systems, the main firm manufacturing these systems, for $775 million. The programmable library stack: books flying and dancing with the help of gentle robotic partners, presenting the reader with generative labyrinths of renewable serendipity.

Outdoor "umbrella" reading room, late 1930s, Multnomah County Library; CC license 2.0.

Libraries of the Here and Now

Few institutions have been more intimately associated in the collective mind with permanence, fixity, and the long-term preservation of knowledge than libraries. Hence the priority that the present essay has granted to their longstanding roles as living mausolea and civic monuments. Hence also the enduring power of such understandings in the collective imagination.

We featured living mausolea and their claustral peers in the lead scenarios of the essay's second half. We then pivoted to consider their digital descendants: the vast and nimble online databases whose impact upon study and learning practices has been driving the worldwide conversation regarding the future of libraries. Next we examined two unconventional, "programmable" formulations of the library as institution, ones that dance back and forth between serving deep time and serving the present. By way of a conclusion, we now turn to the library's past, present, and future civic roles in the here and now.

Many of the questions that arise in this context will, by now, seem familiar. Exactly what kind of civic monument is a

DIYpress — Interlibrary is the name of a kiosk located in public spaces equipped with haptic interfaces that allow data to be searched, collated, remixed, visualized, and combined through print-on-demand into a bespoke volume for the reader. Charges for the service are made directly to the patron's library card. (MB)

library? A monument that serves the living or the dead? A monument to the past, present, or future? What might be gained by supplementing monumental conceptions of the library as civic hub with nimbler or more provisional models of the library as physical place: ones that substitute a devotion to *deep time* with service to the present; ones that deliver libraries to your doorstep, spin off core library functions as freestanding nodes, transform reading spaces into making spaces? What might non- or anti-monumental alternatives to the library have to offer with regard to plausible scenarios for the future as analog collections become entangled with and even sometimes displaced by their digital doubles? What sort of shape might a Library of the Here, the Now, or the Here *and* Now assume? What is its architecture?

In the course of its democratization, the library has increasingly welcomed ordinary citizens, expressions of impermanence, and the noise of contemporary life within its hallowed walls. Its priesthood has multiplied into a legion of professions, from professional librarians to teachers and scholars. Even as it has retained a core commitment to preserving and protecting the human record, it has defined itself as a place devoted to universalizing access to information in the present and fostering the creation of future knowledge.

It is in this spirit that a subset of modern and contemporary library-like structures have sprung up that shun the monumental conception of the library altogether and push out in mobile, present-centered, or local directions, directions that set out to bring information to people instead of people to information, directions that apply pressure to classical notions of study as solitary contemplation or as one that takes place solely in the mausoleum, the monastery, or the mind. The theme of the momentary monument, the monument in motion, and the counter-monument has become a leitmotif of postmodern architecture and design. What of the momentary library, the library in motion, or the library dedicated to making, doing, playing, schooling, inventing?

For all their diversity, instant, counter-, and mobile libraries answer this call. They operate in contexts where the existence of monumental libraries is usually a given, even if unevenly distributed, and the perceived surfeit of information is so great as to necessitate an unexpected site of collection, a novel mode of delivery, or a model of operation centered on making, community building, mobilization for the future. In the following pages we have divided them into three distinct types devoted to the pursuit of *mobility*, to *mobilization*, or to serving *momentary needs*.

Gary, Indiana, public library van with trailer, capable of holding up to 1700 books; from American Library Association, *Book Automobiles*, Library equipment studies, no. 1 (Chicago: The Association, 1937), 39.

Moving

At one end of the spectrum lie efforts to bring services to underserved locations and populations by means of itinerant libraries and mobile book delivery systems. (The latter are, of

Simulibrary – as research libraries migrate toward digital forms, their past is restaged in online simulations that game out all possible research visits to the Vatican Library in the fifteenth century or the Round Reading Room in nineteenth century London. Learning games allow users to retrieve records under varying taxonomical systems. (MB)

course, also integral features of contemporary research libraries that rely upon off-site storage / on-site delivery models.)

The idea of traveling libraries dates back to the eighteenth century. It was first actualized in East Lothian, Scotland in 1817 by Samuel Brown, who set about becoming "one of the agents of the ultimate illumination of the world" by placing books "in the state of perpetual motion over the face of the earth."[56] Inspired as much by evangelical fervor as by Enlightenment ideals, Brown developed a distributed system that was *itinerating* (books rotated from location to location), *cheap* (a single book reached multiple readers), founded upon principles of *self-production* (modest subscription fees covered costs), and *permanence* (the organization was to be sustainable over the course of decades).[57] In his *Memoir Relevant to Itinerant Libraries*, Brown's brother William describes the system as follows:

> The books are formed into divisions of fifty volumes each. One of these divisions is stationed in a place for two years, and the books are issued to all persons above twelve years of age, who will take proper care of them. After that period, it is removed to another town or village, a new division is sent in its place, which, after two years, is again exchanged for another. Thus a perpetual succession of new books is introduced into each town and village.

The result was a collection that toured the East Lothian region in the pursuit of a democratization of access to "the very best literature" and a multiplier effect achieved by limiting the time of availability, thereby fueling desire and demand on the part of patrons. The formula was so successful that it soon spread elsewhere in the United Kingdom, to the continent, and across the Atlantic.

By the Victorian era, the notion of itinerancy had assumed the form of perambulating libraries like the one attested to in *The British Workman*, a journal whose aim it was to "promote the health, wealth, and happiness of the working classes." A February 1, 1857 column notes with approval the presence of:

> a happy looking old man who was wheeling along the high road a novel looking burden. On enquiry, it proved to be the *Perambulating Library*; the large box containing a supply of books which the messenger was taking from Mealsgate to Bolton New Houses. On depositing his burden, he would then have to take the books which had been in use at Bolton New Houses forward to another village, and so on for a circle of *eight* villages, comprising in addition to the above, Ireby, Torpenhow, Bothel, Bolton Low Houses, Sandal, Bolton Gate and Uldale.[58]

The broadsheet goes on to note that "some of our readers may wish to imitate this plan of diffusing good literature amongst the rural population," for which purposes it lists rules that include: the selection of a governing committee, a discerning approach to the books included, the presence of a librarian in every location served, annual dues, and a membership card. Perambulating libraries of smaller and greater dimensions can be documented, among other places, in Cheshire where, at the initiative of the Warrington Mechanics Institute, a book wagon roamed the streets between 1858-1872 greatly dilating the Institute's borrower population.

Perambulating collections had become widespread on both sides of the Atlantic by the first decades of the twentieth century. They had also transitioned from being services associated with subscription libraries or church groups to supporting the outreach efforts of public libraries. Melvil Dewey, the time-traveling hero of the cartoon with which this book opens, was at once the grand synthesizer of a century of prior experiments and the prophet of a new century of books on the move. In his 1901 Home Education Bureau report on the *Field and Future of Traveling Libraries*, he summarized a universe that now included: roaming field librarians; itinerant libraries for study clubs, women, children, and farmers; book wagons; summer hotel libraries; and thematic popup libraries. The reason for this expanded universe was an overall speed-up in the circulation of information: "railways, trolleys, express mail, rural free delivery, telegraphs, cables, telephones, compel us to readjust our ideas in the light of new conditions and possibilities. One result is the traveling library."[59] Dewey concluded: "Libraries must be mobilized. Books must travel more."[60]

And mobilize and travel they did thanks to the American bookmobile movement. Pioneered in 1912 when the first librarian of the Washington County Free Library, Mary Titcomb, took advantage of the International Harvester Autowagon's adaptable chassis to devise the first motorized book truck, capable of transporting two-hundred books, bookmobiles gradually spread from California to upstate New York.[61] By mid-century there were 603 in the United States, with 87 in North Carolina alone. They had also begun to evolve from quirky one-offs into purpose-designed recreational vehicles and trailers sometimes delivering not just books but entire reading rooms and classrooms.[62] The movement reached an initial apex one decade later thanks to passage of the 1956 Library Services Act which provided $40,000 to states that implemented outreach systems for rural areas with populations of 10,000 inhabitants or less. (In 1964 the population restrictions were removed and the LSA also began serving

Alt-libs – popup micro-libraries devoted to the study of evanescent phenomena become a programming arm of the City Central Library. These target seeds, endangered tissues, home movies, discarded photos, found objects, and print ephemera. The most compelling popup projects are promoted for hosting in the Central Library. (JG, JS, MB)

urban districts.) Despite dips in the 1970s and 1980s, growth resumed in the 1990s with over one thousand bookmobiles in operation in such states as Kentucky (110-113 units), Ohio (around 60), and California (around 60).[63] The same number remain in circulation today, some equipped with adaptive technology for the disabled, satellite World Wide Web link-ups, and software and multimedia lending libraries.

In summary, the bookmobile (and the history of experimentation with itinerating/perambulating/traveling collections of which it became the standard bearer) has endured. In the eyes of proponents, it is thriving anew. In the eyes of skeptics, it rumbles down the byways of rural America exuding a halo of anachronism, the icon of a prior era of information delivery. So the abiding question remains: what form could or should bookmobiles assume in the digital age? If libraries as vast as the Library of Congress, the Bibliothèque Nationale de Paris, and the British Library can now be delivered on devices smaller in girth and lesser in heft than a mass market paperback, if bookstores themselves have become the providers of perambulating books, what can be delivered in physical space that cannot be adequately or meaningfully delivered via data networks or fixed-location libraries? To what extent should the deliverables in question be tied to the culture of books or to a print-plus or post-print culture that is still in its infancy? And should today's mobile delivery vectors necessarily favor "the very best literature," whether understood as pious or morally upright materials—the case of most nineteenth century itinerating libraries—or essential knowledge for an educated citizenry—the case of most bookmobiles? Or might they become instead platforms for site-specific, custom tailored, and targeted interventions that address a pressing local circumstance (the presence of a Superfund site, the closure of a factory, a participatory urban planning exercise)?

There are many possible answers to such questions. One that has been implemented in a number of regional contexts is the notion of providing temporary high-speed internet access to underserved areas. However laudable, it is perhaps best viewed as a stopgap measure given the continual growth of wired and wireless networks.

A second reply has deeper roots in the history of bookmobiles. It argues for the distinctiveness of mobile vectors as an outreach tool for fixed-location libraries. The mere existence of collections of tools and resources, whether analog or digital, doesn't guarantee their use, not to mention their *effective* use. So the bookmobile steps in as a novel vector that brings the library directly to potential or actual patrons, breaking down sociocultural barriers and, in the process, establishing library-centric, literate habits. As definitions of literacy come to encompass digital media and technology skills, the vector in question provides even greater value-added when it delivers not just books but the opportunity to interact with otherwise unavailable tools and technologies, as well as expert personnel: all the more so if such expanded notions of literacy are interpreted less in a universal than a local key. In an era where access to "best literature," however defined, is increasingly a given, it is local or regional forms of culture, memory, and knowledge that run the greatest risk of slipping off the grid. So what if the bookmobile were imagined not so much as a universal outreach vector but as a support for knowledge strike forces whose interventions, bounded in time and space, promote community involvement in bringing local knowledge onto the grid by excavating local historical archives, engaging with lost or forgotten local corpora, engaging in local and regional problem solving?

The Internet Archive's Bookmobile project (IAB) enacts a third, forward-looking expression of similar core convictions. The IAB is a bookmobile for the era of networked open source knowledge. Equipped with a satellite uplink, laptops, scanners, a software library that includes readers by Lizard-Tech and Night Kitchen, high-speed color printers, a cutter, and perfect binder, it permits the consultation of online repositories of public domain works and their on-site transformation into bound physical books.[64] A roving "buck a book" production facility capable of yielding four to six bound volumes an hour, it delivers not just product but also process: not just an object you can take home with you but a hands-on experience of the magic of bookmaking (layout, printing, sorting, cutting, and binding).

The IAB example hints at a universe of expanded roles for mobile libraries. The spectrum of such prospects is broad. It could include new sorts of perambulating libraries in the form of home delivery/loan services, much like those provided scholars in research centers, for recondite or non-mainstream categories of literature. It could also include a reinvigoration of bookmobiles: bookmobiles that deliver state-of-the-art hardware tools and software libraries to underserved populations; bookmobiles qua maker spaces where the arts of the book intermingle and mesh with those of contemporary fabrication labs; bookmobiles as digital media training, production, and broadcasting platforms that put the participatory back into participatory media; bookmobiles that serve as a bridge to national digital libraries, facilitating the high-speed scanning and analysis of local collections and archives; or bookmobiles that deliver models of innovation to local public library systems in the form of people, policies, tools, and workshops that can serve as catalysts for self-scrutiny and reinvention or enable site-specific exercises in crisis management, economic retooling, and participatory democracy.

Aleksandr Rodchenko, photograph of USSR Worker's Club installation for USSR Pavilion; from *L'Art décoratif et industriel de l'U.R.S.S.* (Moscow: [s.n.], 1925), 129.

Mobilizing

If placing books in a "state of perpetual motion over the face of the earth" brings library collections out of the stacks into the streets, another set of practices contests traditional definitions of the library as a long-term storehouse. Shunning or sharply delimiting the role of accumulation and storage, they shift the emphasis away from mobile delivery to the mobilizing power of finite, curated information sets brought alive by means of practices of social reading. In the process, the temporal horizons of the library shift as does its architecture. Stacks and shelving systems lose their importance in favor of spaces of activation, conversation, and contemplation such as reading rooms whose duration, rather than being assumed to be perpetual, is determined by the value or utility that a given community ascribes to them.

The reading room has been a standard feature of libraries since antiquity when the porches and gardens adjacent to storage sites were employed for the study and recitation of literary works. During the centuries in which monastic, princely, or patrician libraries prevailed, the very centuries during which the library gradually emerged as a purpose-built architectural environment, the reading room was typically a place of retreat. Labeled a "closet" or "cabinet," a study or *studiolo*, it was intimate in scale and equipped with user-curated temporary shelving or enclosures, furnishings for reading and writing—there was little distinction between the two—and supplies for note-taking, copying, and composition. It was a private space, "social" only to the degree that it supported the exchange of letters and manuscripts with other members of the confraternity of the literate and communion with dead authors.

With the rise of subscription libraries, learned societies, research libraries, and public libraries in the eighteenth and nineteenth centuries, the reading room began to assume its present form. It expanded in scale to the point of becoming the library's showcase and architectural hub: a place of assembly and silent communion for the community of readers, the place of concentration for foundational research assets (dictionaries, reference sets, encyclopedias), the altar of every cathedral of learning. A signal case in point is the British Museum reading room, built in 1854–1857 and frequented by the likes of Karl Marx, Charles Dickens, Arthur Rimbaud, and Virginia Woolf.[65] With its enormous domed vault hung from a cast iron frame, state-of-the-art heating and ventilation systems, and three miles worth of book stacks, it was a circular court presided over by the Principal Librarian, who vetted applications from potential users. Over the course of the subsequent century, reading halls of comparable scale and grandeur will be built in libraries throughout the world from Washington, D.C., to Melbourne.

Despite the migration of reading practices from page to screen, reading rooms have retained their vitality as spaces of retreat and study. But what if reading rooms were detached from the library's traditional collecting and storage functions, so as to become hubs of activity in their own right dedicated less to reading for reading's sake than, for instance, to promoting engagement with a delimited corpus of works for purposes of civic action, social change, or cultural experimentation? What if the rules governing their use were to extend beyond reading qua silent study to embrace a concept of knowledge sharing and creation that includes conversation, performance, public reading, media making, the book arts, and entertainment? And what if the infrastructure, furnishings, equipment, and structure of reading rooms were to be adjusted accordingly, merged with that of spaces of making and recreation?

Such ideas are hardly unprecedented and have long flourished as a complement to library-based reading rooms. In countries such as England and Scotland, freestanding village reading rooms first became popular in the mid-nineteenth century, deriving their inspiration from adult night schools and the evangelization efforts of Bible-study societies. Reform movements promoted them as a sober, character-building alternative to the tavern and public house. To compete with the latter, they were rarely "bookish" in the ordinary sense. They featured games like checkers and chess. Current periodicals were placed on an equal footing with books. They favored conversation as well as silent study, group as well as individual self-improvement. [66]

At the same time that village reading rooms offered a retreat from the workaday world, communities and nations across Europe were awakening to a need for that world's transformation. The Chartist movement, so called for its call to enfranchise the working peoples of Europe through the ratification of "charters" of rights, culminated in 1848 with a series of revolts and mass actions in the capitals of the continent. In many places, barricades were constructed, arms were taken up, and revolt took violent form; in the United Kingdom, progressive discontent simmered at the very edge of rebellion, with tens of thousands taking over public spaces like London's Trafalgar Square. But there was a positive concomitant to these acts of dissidence—and it took the form of libraries. Chartist organizations set up free reading rooms with the purpose of inculcating in their incipient membership a sense of intellectual mission, of curiosity, and critique, from which progressive action might spring. The charters were never passed by Parliament, but the reading room of the Chartists helped to impel and inspire the public library movement that made literacy common among commoners in the second half of the nineteenth century.

A similar concept informed one of the cornerstones of Mary Baker Eddy's Church of Christ Scientist. From the time of the establishment of the first Christian Science reading room in 1888 to the present—they currently number around 2000—the religion's founder envisaged freestanding reading rooms as relays for the dissemination and sale of such works as her own *Science and Health with Key to the Scriptures* and the King James Bible. These were never intended as libraries in the strict sense of the word but, rather, were to be located at busy urban crossroads and kept open during evening hours to encourage browsing, reading, and book purchases as well as consultation of a full array of church publications. Innovative in an era when books were costly and access to them not a given, such reading rooms seem anachronistic today, even if their value for purposes of proselytization has not been lost on successors such as Scientology.

More indicative as regards scenarios for the library's future are the sorts of spaces for socially purposeful or activist reading that may be counted among the legacies of the labor reform movement. Reading rooms for workers have been an article of faith at least since the Victorian age, assuming forms such as Working Men's Institutes, Mechanics' Institutes, and Workers' Self-Help Cooperatives. Though sometimes (too readily) dismissed today as attempts at social control on the part of the privileged, such efforts gave rise to a worldwide workers' club and institute movement, led by progressives like Henry

Solly (1813-1903), as well as to a distinctively new typology of social space. The space in question was built around variations on principles like the following: a society formed on the basis of dues-based memberships within the reach of ordinary working men; worker self-administration; a physical plant where "social intercourse, amusements, and rational recreation [are] the primary object" but always conjoined "to a quiet reading-room and classes for those who wished to improve themselves"; cultural and educational programming including lectures; allowance for consumption of non-alcoholic drinks and smoking; and a socially, politically, and religiously non-sectarian character.[67] In short, the Workers' Club was a kind of coffee house qua library reading room qua school qua union hall.

In the course of its subsequent history, the Working Man's Club undergoes a number of more or less sectarian revisions. One of the more suggestive is the Workers' Club (*Rabochii Klub*) designed as part of the Soviet contribution to the 1925 Exposition Internationale des Arts Décoratifs et Industriels Modernes in Paris by the Russian Constructivist artist, Alexander Rodchenko.[68] Rodchenko's aim was to re-imagine the shabby, dirty, cobbled-together Muscovite early twentieth century descendants of British worker clubs in consonance with the values of Constructivism. The result is a new kind of reading room for a new kind of reader: an austere rectilinear total environment that forsakes luxury in the name of clarity, efficiency, and transparency—an electrified, public, media-rich paradise for the proletariat.

Rodchenko's model workers' club is designed not as a place of leisure and luxury but instead to *mobilize* proletarian bodies and minds. It is a place of action and production, a place for exercising the mind's as well as the body's muscles. Its graphics are clean and dynamic, sharply illuminated by purpose-built angular lighting fixtures. The color scheme is restrained: black, red, gray, and white. The furnishings are simple, functional, un-upholstered. They are comfortable enough to enable reading and sustained discussion but not napping or dawdling.

Books are present in Rodchenko's reading room but they no longer rule the roost. Immersed in a present-centered information ecology, they are outflanked by posters, magazines, and daily newspapers. All are tilted toward the reader as if to say: "I am within reach"; "I'm not an object of worship"; "I'm here to be read (not stored)"; "I am an industrially produced artifact, replaceable, and renewable." Similarly, the wings of the main reading table hinge symmetrically, promoting the activity of reading rather than the passive display of documents in their inclined position. In the Lenin corner, there are moveable wall cases for posters, banners ready to be carried out into the streets, and banks of up-to-the-minute photographs displayed in rotating hexagonal cases. An expansible/collapsible speaker's rostrum with pull-out screen flanks the entrance, designed to serve as the focal point for rallies and performances of living newsreels. There is room for play in Rodchenko's productivist paradise, but serious, mind-stretching play: a revolving chess board spins between two conjoined chairs equipped with storage boxes for the chess pieces. In short, the Constructivist workers' club is a social space that merges elements of the library, school, factory, laboratory, cinema, and public square.

Libraries have long been all (or most) of the above, whether inspired by visions of a society tilting to the left, center, or right. In addition to book stacks, Andrew Carnegie's first American library, built in Braddock, Pennsylvania in 1889, included a gymnasium, music hall, and swimming pool. Angus Snead Macdonald's 1933 Library of the Future, whose interior and exterior architecture is designed to establish "a feeling of homelike intimacy rather than monumental impressiveness" so as to invite active usage by all social classes, was no less comprehensive in its architectural program. It featured materials libraries and workshops alongside clusters of moveable book stacks, recording studios for music and film, children's activity spaces, a day-care facility, a movie theater and stage, a fountain, pool, and outdoor café, all accompanied by a roof garden that served as a "demonstrating laboratory for the Home Gardens department."[69] Tea was to be served in the entrance lobby, so as to convey an air of informal simplicity, of club-like comfort immune to elitist fussiness.

Not unlike such immediate predecessors and successors, early twentieth century efforts like Rodchenko's to imagine new sorts of spaces for social reading inspire scenarios for the present and future that apply pressure to once fundamental hierarchies, like the subordination of the hand to the mind, manual to mental modes of inquiry, the applied to the theoretical. Prominent among these scenarios is the notion of freestanding reading rooms as civic making spaces variously instanced in recent experiments with popup maker spaces located outside or within existing library facilities (as in the case of the 4th floor of the Chattanooga Public Library).[70] Such redesigns build on and, indeed, radicalize the idea of the library as a place of action, production, and purposeful play, insisting upon an expanded understanding of intellectual labor that encompasses classically understood reading, writing, and study, the practice of digitally and non-digitally inflected forms of craft, and production work with old and new media.

Informed by a similar spirit, Idea Stores have arisen as an effort to reshape some of the capabilities of traditional libraries around a core set of community service commitments: to education, training, recreation, and social outreach. Elaborated in 1999 on the basis of a wide-ranging opinion survey of the London Borough of Tower Hamlets, the concept was first translated into a physical plant by the architect David Adaye at Chrisp Street and Whitechapel Road in the form of blue and green

Drone Library – a booksharing platform is served by drones powered to carry books over short distances. The drones fly a pattern in search of a building with a lib-landing pad kitted out with machine-readable targeting info. After docking, the subscriber can unload one book and replace it with another, at which point the drone flies off in search of a new borrower. (MB, NR)

glass-walled structures designed to reflect and interconnect with the awnings of the marketplace that surrounds both sites. The buildings' interiors differ slightly, but both privilege activity spaces over storage, granting them a visibility on all floors that disallows for so-called dead spaces. Shelves and desks are integrated into each building's structural system and façade. In what amounts to an allegory of the Idea Store as community, every component of the building can be seen to be supporting another. Developed with funding from the British Secretary of State for the Department of Culture, Media, and Sport, the first Idea Store was built in Bow in 2002, followed by Chrisp Street in 2004. Next came Whitechapel in 2005, the system's flagship facility. Two additional units have been built since that time: Canary Wharf (2006) and Whatney Market (2013).

Such programs can have a dramatic impact in precarious global contexts, even when implemented on a modest scale. Rio de Janeiro's Biblioteca Parque de Manguinhos provides a compelling case in point. Located on a plain in Rio's Zone Norte, far from the famous beaches and verdant mountain vistas, Manguinhos is a vast archipelago of favela neighborhoods (including the Coreia, Mandela, and Amorim slums) marked by desperate poverty, elevated lead levels, a lack of public services, and the strife of warring drug-trafficking factions. Five years ago, the state of Rio de Janeiro funded the development of a 25,000 square foot library on the site of a former army outpost. Situated between warring favelas, the Biblioteca Parque de Manguinhos was inaugurated in April 2010. It was designed with panoramic windows opening out on both communities to foster a sense of interconnection. It offers not only books and broadband access, but a suite of cultural infrastructure features not often found in libraries, including classrooms, a literary café, a movie theater, a large black-box theater, and a music room outfitted with drums, horns, and stringed instruments. Such affordances provide Manguinhos residents with the opportunity to activate connected learning in material contexts. It doesn't help much to have access to dramatic literature without a stage to put scripts into production; YouTube may offer myriad instructional videos in guitar or electric keyboards, but such instruments are typically beyond the means of favela residents.

In addition to its services and features, the Biblioteca Parque de Manguinhos invites users to experiment with models of civic participation and institutional engagement previously unimaginable in the favelas' unincorporated, feral world. Residents man the check-in desks, shelve the books, and run the media services. In the library, the state and city manifest themselves not as the agents of repression once present in the guise of a military emplacement, but as functional and supportive adjuncts to daily life. The spirit of possibility is expressed in the form of friendly library rules, posted at the front door. Instead of proscribing prohibited behaviors, these enumerate things that *can* be done in the library. "Here, you can wear clothes in your style," the sign says; "you can bring your cell phone… and you can talk!" The Manguinhos library is "founded on the notion that libraries shouldn't just be silent spaces, but places akin to freely accessible cultural centers."[71] Both the overall tone and the substance of its programming (centered on promoting literacy and facilitating access to cultural resources) mark a dramatic break with respect to the harsh ways in which state authority has typically manifested itself in the favelas. And the message is spreading: a second state-funded library opened this year in Rocinha, a favela in Rio's Zona Sul, with a third slated to open by the end of 2013 in the Complexo do Alemão.

The civic vision that animates Idea Stores and the Biblioteca Parque de Manguinhos has greater potential than could have been understood back in 1999 or even 2010, given that the migration of document forms online has been accompanied by an explosion of online learning forums, from instructional video channels to academies (Khan Academy) to, most recently, massive open online courses (MOOCs). Such online delivery platforms promise to democratize access to high quality information and reduce the costs. But they do so at the expense of the social and cultural dimensions of learning: a loss that translates into high incompletion rates, impoverished models of interaction, a lack of cohort-building and context, not to mention diminished attention to complexities that don't readily translate to machine logics or to the screen. The result has been a growing attention to hybrid learning models that link the online to the physical classroom, telepresence with interactions that take place face-to-face.

So now imagine constellations of networked "reading rooms," equipped to serve as state-of-the-art study and research centers combining topic-specific digital devices and media, expert personnel to serve as teachers, project leaders, and managers; and analog resources borrowed from partner institutions, whether libraries and archives or local historical associations, selected on a project-by-project basis.[72] Free from the constraints of scholastic calendars, able to interact with a plurality of institutional actors, from government to universities and schools to museums and concert halls to the private sector, such spaces would be programmable on multiple time scales. They could leverage online curricula in strategic, locally determined ways for a variety of purposes, from vocational training, lifelong learning, and the expansion of school curricula to local problem solving to play and exploration to supporting citizen science and participatory history projects. And they could be organized at once like classrooms, with recurring periods of formal or informal group face-to-face interaction, and like laboratories where participants can also interact on a frequent basis within the setting of an ongoing group project.[73]

The disadvantages of such an approach may include elevated costs, the complexities of administering and programming flexible multiuse spaces and institutional partnerships, and the challenge of ensuring sustained participation and visibility. The advantages are multiple: it builds on existing infrastructures rather than adding redundant resources, expands the capabilities of individual institutional actors within a community, and builds bridges between institutions in new and productive ways.

People's Library, Occupy Wall Street, Nov. 12, 2011; photograph by David Shankbone (Occupy Wall Street Creative Commons Project); CC license 2.0.

Momentary

If mobile libraries shift the focus away from the library as a fixed physical hub toward ubiquitous, even personalized delivery systems, and mobilizing libraries multiply the library's roles as a knowledge activation and production center while downplaying the importance of information storage, the momentary library makes a virtue of impermanence. It furnishes an event-driven complement or alternative to the library as civic monument and social actor. It nurtures counter-memories, harbors protest movements, provides a haven for emer-

Abject Library — a shareable, crowd-curated library of e-books deemed to be abject is delivered via text messages. Content contributors whose work receives the "most abject" rating are promoted to "master of abjection" status. (JS, MB)

gent or evanescent forms of thought and culture (that may or may not emerge or evanesce). Because the event's the thing, it worries less about product than process.

Momentary libraries have less history than their mobile counterparts, but they are the first cousins of mobilizing libraries. They seek to bind together information and conversation with action in the form of making, experimentation, and social action. They typically arise in a limited set of circumstances and against the backdrop of an existing brick-and-mortar library system: either as a result of a sense of crisis, the perceived need to provide a focal point for an otherwise dispersed or invisible community, or out of a sense of opportunity, particularly in the setting of special events such as conferences and festivals.

The first model is best exemplified by popup institutions like the tent libraries that sprung up within the encampments that characterized the initial phase of the Occupy movement (much as they once were present at 1970s sit-ins and Chartist reading rooms a century before). These were spontaneous and relatively rudimentary initiatives aimed at the bottom-up creation of a tightly curated corpus of materials in support of the Occupy movement: a counter-library whose core was drawn from works present in the stacks of standard libraries, but here featured in an environment where the collection was framed by pressing questions of political practice. The counter-canon thus constructed was eclectic. It included classic works of cultural criticism and radical theory, borrowings from lost and abandoned traditions of activism (particularly of anarchist and pacifist derivation), digital media, and print ephemera in the form of camp pamphlets and samizdat-type literature.

Not unlike tent libraries, popup "libraries" dedicated to supporting subcultures that usually fall outside the collecting practices of conventional libraries such as zines, chapbooks, or nonmainstream music serve as community-building devices. Like

Lend-to-Own Library – a library and bookstore merge so that every book in the stacks is available for lending as well as purchase. If a borrowed book is retained beyond 48 hours, it has been bought. The lender is charged; a replacement is ordered. (N.b. – this system was tried out at CalArts in the early 1970s.) (JS)

their "mobilizing" cousins, they emphasize support of the creative process as much as gathering, collecting, documenting, and sharing otherwise disaggregated, marginal, or invisible materials. Such intertwined acts of collecting, sharing, and making are typically sustained by communities of practitioners (and not addressed to outsiders). Their location and time horizon are dictated by practitioner habits rather than the needs of a user community.

At the furthest end of the spectrum of ephemerality lie experiments such as the Harvard LABrary and the informal library-like salons that have become a recurring feature at idea festivals and conferences like SXSW (South by Southwest). Informed less by a sense of urgency than of opportunity, such ventures merge many of the features of the tent and community-of-practitioners popup library with those of makers' fairs and salons, seeking to incubate a culture of innovation and experimentation, to build community, to foster dialogue and cross-pollination. Here, rather than constructing counter-canons or reconstructing lost or marginal histories, the emphasis falls on emerging thinking in ways that favor live or ephemeral media and place print in a subordinate relation.

The LABrary weaves together many of the aforementioned threads. Developed in a storefront location in Harvard Square in October through December of 2012, it assumed the form of a hybrid event-space, design studio, and open classroom dedicated to exploring future scenarios for libraries. The initiative came about on the heels of a several years of developments that were instrumental in the genesis of the present book: public discussion of the ongoing reorganization of the Harvard University library system, the establishment of the Harvard Library Lab with support from the Arcadia Foundation, and the launch of the Digital Public Library of America in the midst of a creeping sense of uncertainty regarding the mission of brick-and-mortar traditional libraries. It was directly instigated, however, by a two-year-long design studio, initially entitled *Bibliotheca*, subsequently *Library Test Kitchen*, devoted to building the library of the future "one component at time" by means of a series of speculative, but historically informed design exercises.[74] So, the LABrary was, in the first instance, a workshop housing student experiments: a reading room in the form of a reflective mylar inflatable; prototypes for reading tables and conical reading shelters; an oral history project on library experiences; a spiral column made out of books; usable collections of old media devices (viz. typewriters). It was also a space programmed for well-informed public conversations regarding policy, planning, and design involving not just librarians, faculty, and students from a variety of Harvard schools, but also public libraries and librarians as well as ordinary citizens.

However intriguing, momentary libraries represent less a plausible vision of the future than models for how one might expand the library's institutional contours in order to address a number of emerging cultural and societal needs and opportunities. The library's traditional mission as a storehouse of knowledge, its universal vocation as a site of study, rumination, and knowledge gathering, remain more pertinent than ever in a knowledge economy. But as models of discovery, access, and activation continue to diversify there is a need less to replace than to reinforce the library as civic monument by *multiplying its component parts.* And it is here that momentary libraries, not to mention their mobile and mobilizing peers, help to fuel the imagination. The challenge is that of proliferating the library's organs in productive ways. To distribute them amidst the cityscape by means of temporary as well as enduring site- and occasion-specific appendages whose purpose and values may sometimes be in tension with the library's universal or long-term aims but that, nonetheless, contribute other forms of value, inclusiveness, and variety.

Arielle Assouline-Lichten & Gabrielle Patawaran, LABrary, Cambridge, MA, Nov. 2012 (photo by Jeff Goldenson)

Ben Brady, inflatable mylar reading room, LABrary, Cambridge, MA, Nov. 2012 (photo by Arielle Assouline-Lichten)

Ben Brady, cold spot signage in laser cut plastic, Library Test Kitchen, spring 2012 (photo by Ben Brady)

James Bridle talk, Nov. 13, 2012; LABrary, Cambridge, MA, (photo by Jeff Goldenson)

Ben Brady, Meet Biblio, Your Library Friend; Library Test Kitchen, spring 2012 (photo by Ben Brady)

Hattie Stroud, Topical Table with programmable sound distraction level, LABrary, Cambridge, MA, Nov. 2012 (photo by Hattie Stroud)

So...

Prognostication is a fool's game. Recall the meretricious forecast made by Melvil Dewey's companion in the comic strip in the first pages of the book: "the literature of the future might turn out to be the daily exchange of ideas … over the everlasting telephone."[75] As noted in the strip, the wag's words derive from an actual prognosis offered in a letter to Isabella Stewart Gardner in the early twentieth century. It joins a distinguished lineage of fatally flawed forecasts: the Chief Engineer of the British Post Office, Sir William Preece, declaring in 1878 that "the Americans have need of the telephone, but we do not [because] we have plenty of messenger boys"; Guglielmo Marconi predicting in 1912 that "the coming of the wireless era will make war impossible because it will make war ridiculous"; and a veritable swarm of digital-age descendants, from the IBM Corporation's 1959 assertion that the potential global market for copying machines would never exceed 5,000 units to Steve Ballmer's 2007 wholesale dismissal of the iPhone's potential impact on the cellular telephone market.[76] Who could say with certainty that any of these statements were mistaken, given the information available at the time? The mistake consists in making a prediction.

We cast our Melvil Dewey in the role of a steampunk time-traveler; perhaps it's time to unpack the gesture. Steampunk, after all, is one of the more expressive and problematic cultural irruptions of the networked age. At its worst, it sanitizes the early industrial era, effacing its awful effects—large-scale pollution, the systematic exploitation of labor, the rise of colonialism and a rapacious oligarchy—in favor of an always gleaming brass-and-clockwork romance. At its best, however, it offers a playful and inventive critique of the wages of industrialization, imagining a world in which science and technology are mobilized for personal empowerment, not exploitation and control; in which mechanico-digital "difference engines" calculate without alienation and depersonalization; and in which the otherwise-invisible forces of the digital age are translated retroactively into the clattering, hissing, visible vernacular of the old analog machinery. "Love the machine, hate the factory," goes a favored steampunk maxim[77]—a sentiment that would have made sense to William Morris. Like the Arts and Crafts movement, steampunk disassembles the past and puts it to use as a toy chest or kit of parts: less to propose alternative futures than to critique and remodel the present.[78] Like camp, steampunk appropriates exploitative forms, knitting them together in a reverie of liberation never entirely immune to the temptation of anachronism tinted with nostalgia.

In this sense, libraries in Dewey's era—the late nineteenth century, steampunk's mythic dream time—were themselves difference engines of a kind. However imperfectly, the public library movement Dewey led championed a kind of institution that appropriated elite patterns of bookish behavior and architectures of privilege on behalf of popular sovereignty and democratic assimilation. While the ethics of the public library movement may have sometimes proven troublingly paternalistic and libertarian, it came closer than any other progressive-era effort to offering a vaunted species of intellectual and spiritual emancipation that modernity has often honored only in the breach.

Like a good steampunk, Dewey expressed this ethos in terms of gadgets. While best remembered for the material epistemology of his Decimal Classification System, his contemporary impact was felt largely through the inventive line of furniture and fittings he peddled through the catalogs of his supply company, The Library Bureau.[79] As much as any innovation in lending policies or cataloging practices, Dewey's bookshelves, reference desks, and copy presses redirected the exclusionary and elite energies of prior libraries into popular terms. The ethos of invention and innovation that they embodied transformed the once predictable patrician world of traditional library fittings, devices, and office supplies into an industrial wonderland populated by Lever Self-Inkers, Universal Binders, Ventilated Eye-Shades, Hectographs, Ink Vents, Date-Stamp equipped pens, whirling Wire Atlas Stands, and nimble Book Trucks. Here we encounter one of the most fertile of foundations on which to

erect the Library Labs and Library Test Kitchens of a historical present beyond the book. By hacking and recombining
the furnishings of the library, we also reimagine its social
and cultural ties to the contemporary world.[80]

What we seek, in the end, is a way of talking about what
libraries are and what they do that is flexible with respect to
site, materiality, and social context; that catalyzes a new library culture of digitally inflected play, invention, and imagination. Steampunk, Arts and Crafts, the public library movement—these gestures, already related in terms of their historical and cultural antecedents, perhaps have in common the
qualities of a pattern language.[81] In *The Library Beyond the
Book*, we've identified a few of the words in that pattern language—ways of thinking through the perils and possibilities
of library design suited to the ever-emergent present, which
are flexible, innovative, remixable, and intuitively accessible.
And not only to librarians, but to communities of readers
and writers, information consumers and producers (such
distinctions have attenuated over recent decades). We've ges-
tured toward a vocabulary for such a pattern language, in the
cases, types, and historical sketches proposed above. But what
of grammar and syntax? How do such typologies and exem-
pla combine to form patterns that describe the new ways libraries want to be in the world?

What we are after is the kind of flexibility and inven-
tiveness John Ruskin cited in describing the qualities of the
gothic style:

> Undefined in its slope of roof, height of shaft, breadth of
> arch, or disposition of ground plan, it can shrink into a
> turret, expand into a hall, coil into a staircase, or spring
> into a spire, with undegraded grace and unexhausted
> energy; and whenever it finds occasion for change in its

form or purpose, it submits to it without the slightest sense
of loss either to its unity or majesty,—subtle and flexible
like a fiery serpent, but ever attentive to the voice of the
charmer.[82]

In like fashion, we have sought to conjure up flexible,
case-dependent, community-inspired libraries capable of
reimagining both themselves and the very technologies upon
which they have come to rely: places where an accumulibrary
can shrink into a mobile library, expand into a database, coil
into a cloister, or spring into a material epistemology like a
fiery viper ever attentive to the voice of a collectivity.

We're sliding among marginally reputable cultural gestures, from steampunk to the gothic … it was after all the
champion of a renascent gothic who coined the watchword of
the modern open-stack library: serendipity. We are surrounded by libraries many of which don't bear the moniker library.
Like the Princes of Serendip in Horace Walpole's tale,[83] we
need to develop the sagacity to recognize when we are in their
midst and to draw inspiration from these non-library libraries
in staging an imaginative leap toward plausible futures.

Of course, humanity long ago recognized the metaphorical power of the library to denominate the properties of
intelligence, memory, and accumulation; a "walking library"
is someone whose knowledge we find capacious and trust-
worthy. But in a world whose informational properties are
increasingly indexed and operationalized, everything strives
to express a latent bibliothecality. Looking across at the new-
ly-shingled gable visible through the office window, one sees
the concentric arcs of tree rings in the yet-unpainted wood: a
dendrochronological library, uncataloged, registering the tale
of the lost trees' years. The web is a library, indeed. But so is a
tree, a crowd, and an individual (the latter increasingly less

for the knowledge in her head than for the information in her genome—and not only her own genome, but those of the microbial fauna that share her person, along with her online clicks, the graph of her social networks, the concentric aureoles formed by everything from the archive of her logged GPS locations to her text messaging repository to her lifelong inventory of emails). How to bring out the experience- and wisdom-laden qualities of these immanent non-library libraries while retaining community, autonomy, privacy, and civic agency? How might one design or build a house of wisdom where these qualities can live a thriving life as well as a flourishing afterlife?

In the early years of phonographic technology, Rainer Maria Rilke described with surprise the similarity between scratches made upon wax cylinders in the recording process and the contours of the coronal suture, that vermiform line connecting the temples where the parietal and frontal bones of the skull meet:

> What if one changed the needle and directed it on its
> return journey … along the coronal suture, for example.
> What would happen? A sound would necessarily result,
> a series of sounds, music…
>
> Feelings—which? Incredulity, timidity, fear, awe—which of
> all the feelings here possible prevents me from suggesting
> a name for the primal sound which would then make its
> appearance in the world…
>
> Leaving that aside for a moment: what variety of lines then,
> occurring anywhere, could one not put under the needle
> and try out? Is there any contour that one could not,
> in a sense, complete in this way and then experience it, as

Library of Lost Tongues – a storehouse for texts in dead and dying languages organized according to a taxonomical scheme whose encryption key has been lost. The construction of the library of lost tongues is gamified to reward the most imaginative reconstructions of the "original" organizational scheme. (JS, MB)

it makes itself felt, thus transformed, in another field of
sense?[84]

In the era of the analog machine, Rilke intuited digital technology's capacity for making apparent the strange music bot-
tled up at the sutures and seams of the world. Now, these
ubiquitous data emerge from every pore and tangle in the
world in analysis-prone profusion. And so it is in the library
a fortiori, where acts of data-consumption produce more
data. Every time a book is taken off the shelf, a file is down-
loaded, or a computer work station is booted up, a story is
told, and cataloged, and filed away in a database. In this way,
each act of reading in the library broadcasts a handful of
seeds, from which new growths of data will either spring—or
disappear into a forest of statistical noise.

In a recent interview, the writer Neil Gaiman affirmed
the importance of librarians in the midst of this tangled bank
of information:

> We've gone from looking at a desert, in which a librarian
> had to walk into the desert for you and come back with a
> lump of gold, to a forest, to this huge jungle in which what
> you want is one apple. And at that point, the librarian can
> walk into the jungle and come back with the apple. So I
> think from that point of view, the time of librarians, and the
> time of libraries—they definitely haven't gone anywhere.[85]

Metaphors are figures of transport from the known to the
unknown and Gaiman's propose an intuitively appealing formula for the library vocation in the digital era: from prospec-
tor to forest guide. An image that comes to mind in connection with the librarian-guide is the "Stalker" in Andrei Tarkovsky's film of the same name. Played by a mournful Alex-

ander Kaidanovsky, the Stalker is a guide to the "Zone": a mysterious region in which some undefined event—a disaster, a miracle, an alien invasion—has taken place, leaving a region thick with traces of power and danger, with no clear markers to divide one from the other. People make their way to the Zone seeking to experience this power, despite mortal threats that hover unseen. And the Stalker is one who—having denied himself access to the force in a vow of self-abnegation—devotes his life to showing others how to negotiate the Zone's hidden mysteries and invisible wonders.

The Stalker is a guide to a ruined world: less a tragic figure than one who is morbid and absurd. Perhaps he's the avatar of those who mourn the materiality of books and libraries past. But the Zone is not the world in its entirety. At most, it's a harbinger of what the world could become were the disaster to become universal. Even the Stalker knows that by focusing on ruin and danger alone, the Zone's wonder will prove elusive.

We want this Zone to yield up its mysteries. But we want more. We want to know the sources of mystery, how to incorporate its savor into our lives with imagination—and to discern which wonders, despite their alluring aspect, may prove fatal in the long run. We wish to become Stalkers ourselves. In Gaiman's jungle, we desire the apples, but we need good recipes as well. If the new kind of librarian is a forest guide, then perhaps we are all gatherers and cooks, whose desire is to serve up a bountiful banquet of story and data, knowledge and information.

So, alongside Gaiman's explorer and Tarkovsky's Stalker, let's add one final metaphorical role: that of the cook. As we enter the third year of the Library Test Kitchen design studio, the power and force of this metaphor has become ever clearer. Each time it has unfolded, the Test Kitchen has fostered conversation about libraries within a larger and more diverse community. It has invited librarians, students, academics, storekeepers, young people, and walk-in members of the public to come together over a hot stove, tossing new and old ingredients together to see what kinds of new recipes for the library beyond the book might emerge. It has fostered the kind of antic, propositional spirit found when friends whip something up together: dishes with a zestier flavor than that of the dour end-of-the-book pronouncements found in too many contemporary ruminations on the library's future. And this spirit is about to escape the Library Test Kitchen and hit the road, whether in the form of the present book or in that of a library "innovation strike force" van: the principal design project on the agenda for the fall semester of 2013–2014. Think of it as a food truck for the library beyond the book.

From the Mausoleum to the Pop-up Book Room, the patterns identified in *The Library Beyond the Book* are merely so many ingredients. As we meet and mix in libraries—some without books, others without walls—we must learn to re-imagine these still-thriving institutions in a spirit of openness and experimentation. It's pot luck. Everybody has flavors to bring to the table, whether in the form of produce from their gardens, rare spices from the cupboard, new techniques or time-tested family recipes. We've presented a library of such flavors in the course of these pages, dreamed up in a kitchen that draws its sustenance from history and tradition even as it looks beyond.

Rola Idris & Pablo Roquero, Mille Books
and Graham Grams (a printing system for
edible books), Library Test Kitchen project,
Nov. 2012 (photos by Jeff Goldenson)

Endnotes

1   As **Walter J. Ong** points out with some frequency in *Orality and Literacy* (Oxford: Routledge, 2002), "writing restructures consciousness"; in similar fashion, it becomes impossible to grasp the print book except through the lens of digital culture and the changes in consciousness it has already wrought.

2   On the subject of Snead stack systems, the systems employed at NYPL and Widener, see **Snead and Company Iron Works**, *Library Planning, Bookstacks and Shelving with Contributions from Architects and Librarians' Points of View* (Stamford, CT: Architecture Press, 1915), but also **Charles H. Baumann**, *The Influence of Angus Snead MacDonald and the Snead Bookstack on Library Architecture* (Metuchen, N.J.: Scarecrow Press, 1972). For a full listing of buildings built using Snead systems see Appendix III, 266-84.

3   Anonymous, "New York's Great Public Library Nearing Completion: A Huge Bookcase to Hold 4,500,000 Volumes," *New York Times Sunday Magazine* (October 1, 1905): 4. The stacks themselves were forged by Snead & Company Iron Works in Jersey City, New Jersey. NYPL opened its doors to the public in 1911. Inaugurated in 1915, Widener Library was designed by Horace Trumbauer & Associates to similar specifications, on which subject one may consult **Matthew Battles**, *Widener: Biography of a Library* (Cambridge, MA: Harvard University Libraries, 2004).

4   As a case in point, see **Ross Dawson**'s *Extinction Timeline* on his "Trends in the Living Networks" blog which, as far back as October 14, 2007 was proclaiming the disappearance of libraries in 2019, preceded by the disappearance of "getting lost" in 2014 and retirement in 2016, and followed by the disappearance of copyright in 2020 and glaciers in 2037. http://rossdawsonblog.com/weblog/archives/2007/10/extinction_time.html, accessed Sept. 6, 2013.

5   **Catullus**, Poem 1 ("cui dono lepidum novum libellum"), translation by authors. Catullus refers to his work as a *libellum*, an indication of the lyric's lesser status as well as a gesture of humility; his word for the work's ideal duration is *saeculum*, a word rich with meanings encompassing a lifetime, one hundred years, or an entire historical epoch.

6   **Alan Liu** has written on this topic in "Transcendental Data – Toward a Cultural History and Aesthetics of the New Encoded Discourse," pp. 209-36 in *Local Transcendence: Essays on Postmodern Historicism and the Database* (Chicago and London: University of Chicago Press, 2008).

7   Cited from http://booktwo.org/notebook/new-aesthetic-politics/.

8   **Strabo**, *Geographica* 17.1.8 C 793-4 cited from **Gregory Nagy**, *The Idea of the Library as a Classical Model for European Culture*, http://chs.harvard.edu/wa/pageR?tn=ArticleWrapper&bdc=12&mn=3999#n.13.

9   We have in mind the passage in *Phaedrus* 275b-277a in which **Socrates** contrasts the "living speech" of dialectic with the "dead discourse" of writing.

10 **Charles C. Soule**, *Library Journal* 16 (Dec. 1891): 17-19. It is perhaps worth noting that Soule went on to publish his own guidebook for architects: *How to Plan a Library Building for Library Work* (Boston:

Boston Book Co., 1912).

11 In fact the aphorism has been attributed to the twelfth-century neoplatonist **Bernard of Chartres**, who spoke with reference to the classical *auctores*.

12 On this general topic see **Lionel Casson**, *Libraries in the Ancient World* (New Haven: Yale University Press, 2001). We have also consulted **Jason König, Katerina Oikonomopoulou, Greg Woolf**, eds., *Ancient Libraries* (Cambridge: Cambridge University Press, 2013).

13 **Christopher Alexander**, *A Pattern Language: Towns, Buildings, Construction* (Oxford: Oxford University Press, 1977).

14 **R. David Lankes**, *The Atlas of New Librarianship* (Cambridge, MA: MIT Press, 2011).

15 **Francis Bacon**, *The Advancement of Learning* 2.4, cited from the Project Gutenberg digital edition of the 1893 Cassell & Company printing, http://www.gutenberg.org/cache/epub/5500/pg5500.txt.

16 *The Advancement of Learning* 2.5.

17 A concise overview of the modern history of library building types may be found in **Walter C. Allen,** "Library Buildings," *Library Trends* 25 (July 1976): 89-112.

18 In "A Paean to Paper," **Robert Darnton** has outlined some of the arguments in favor of the preservation of paper copies with respect to paper originals; our argument extends that notion to paper backups of digital originals. See Darnton, *The Case for Books. Past, Present, and Future* (New York: Public Affairs, 2009), 109-30.

19 Here as elsewhere in the present essay, there are affinities between our scenarios and the genealogy from libraries to monasteries and universities to laboratories traced in **Ian F. McNeely** and **Lisa**

Wolverton's *Reinventing Knowledge from Alexandria to the Internet* (New York: Norton, 2008).

20 On Cassiodorus, see **James J. O'Donnell**, *Cassiodorus* (Berkeley and Los Angeles: University of California Press, 1979).

21 The episode is detailed in O'Donnell, *Cassiodorus*, 182-5.

22 The building of the Vivarium's library collections is discussed in O'Donnell, *Cassiodorus*, 192-3, 218-22.

23 **Lellia Cracco Ruggini**, "Cassiodorus and the Practical Sciences," in **Samuel Barnish** et al., *Vivarium in Context* (Vicenza: Centre for Medieval Studies Leonard Boyle, 2008), 23.

24 **Samuel Rolles Driver**, ed. *Studies in Biblical and Patristic Criticism: or, Studia Biblica et Ecclesiastica* (Piscataway, NJ: Gorgias Press, 2006; facsimile ed.; series Oxford 1885).

25 **Thomas Hughes**, *Scouring of the White Horse* (Boston: Ticknor and Field, 1859), 37-8.

26 **Stuart Schieber**, "The Scouring of the White Horse," blog post (http://blogs.law.harvard.edu/pamphlet/2011/04/18/the-scouring-of-the-white-horse/, accessed 7/9/2013).

27 **Stewart Brand**, *The Clock of the Long Now: Time and Responsibility* (New York: Basic Books, 1999), 3.

28 See chapter six ("The Monastic Quadrangle and Collegiate Ideals") in **Paul Venable Turner**, *Campus, An American Planning Tradition* (Cambridge, MA and London, England: MIT Press; New York: Architectural History Foundation, 1984), 215-48.

29 **Charles Rufus Morey**, *A Laboratory-Library* (Princeton: Princeton University Store, 1932). This pamphlet, printed at

Morey's own expense and complete with floor plans, goes on to call for the transformation of the library into a full-blown "humanistic laboratory." It represents Morey's polemical intervention on the subject of a campus debate regarding designs for a new university library. Some of Morey's points were eventually adopted in the design of Firestone Library, inaugurated in 1948.

30 **Jorge Luis Borges**, "On Exactitude in Science" ("Del rigor en la ciencia"; 1946), trans. Andrew Hurley, cited from http://www.sccs.swarthmore.edu/users/08/bblonder/phys120/docs/borges.pdf.

31 **Tony Campbell**, "Portolan Charts from the Late Thirteenth Century to 1500," in *The History of Cartography, Volume One (Cartography in Prehistoric, Ancient, and Medieval Europe and the Mediterranean)*, ed. by J. B. Hartley and David Woodward (Chicago: University of Chicago Press, 1987).

32 **Lev Manovich**, *Language of New Media* (Cambridge, MA: MIT Press, 2002), 197-8.

33 Manovich, *Language of New Media*, 198.

34 **Elizabeth Eisenstein**, *Printing Revolution in Early Modern Europe* (Cambridge: Cambridge University Press, 1983).

35 Eisenstein, *Printing Revolution in Early Modern Europe*, 223.

36 **Ann Blair**, *Too Much to Know: Managing Scholarly Information Before the Modern Age* (New Haven: Yale University Press, 2011).

37 The passage is from the preamble to René Descartes, *Recherches de la vérité par les lumières naturelles* cited in Blair, *Too Much to Know*, 5.

38 "Letter 2," **Lucius Annaeus Seneca**, *Letters from a Stoic*, trans. Robin Campbell, the Penguin Classics (New York and London: Penguin Books, 1969), 33. The Latin original of the final phrase is "distringit librorum multitudo."

39 **Edward Hutchins**, *Cognition in the Wild* (Cambridge, MA: MIT Press, 1995). Hutchins's ethnography of navigation on ships of the United States Navy offers an evocative account of knowledge produced and persisting amidst naval officers and noncoms, "in the air" as it were, embodied tools, protocols, and even the command structure.

40 **David Weinberger**, "Library as Platform," *Library Journal*, September 24, 2012, cited from http://lj.libraryjournal.com/2012/09/future-of-libraries/by-david-weinberger/#_, accessed July 17, 2013.

41 http://www.europeana.eu/.

42 http://trove.nla.gov.au/general/api.

43 You may not be a code-savvy user, but it's likely that you know one—at least if you're reading this book. One of the allied dynamics of the library-as-database is the impetus it lends to collaborative use: one user will have a research question and the hard-won domain expertise, another the technological know-how to express answers in dynamic new-media form. We're connected to one another through social networks old and new; reach out and find someone to teach, and to learn from.

44 Weinberger, "Library as Platform."

45 On this subject see **Angela Nuovo**, *The Book Trade in the Italian Renaissance* (Leiden and Boston: Brill, 2013), particularly chapter 4 (pp. 117-42).

46 **Comte de Lautréamont**, *Lautréamont's Maldoror*, trans. by Alexis Lykiard (New York: Thomas Y. Crowell, 1972), 177.

47 **Jorge Luis Borges**, "The Total Library," from *Selected Non-Fictions*, ed. Eliot

Weinberger, trans. Esther Allen, Suzanne Jill Levine and Eliot Weinberger (New York: Viking, 1999), 216.

48 "The books are not yet on the shelves, not yet touched by the mild boredom of order." **Walter Benjamin**, "Unpacking My Library – A Talk about Book Collecting," *Illuminations*, ed. Hannah Arendt, trans. Harry Zohn (New York: Schocken Books, 1968), 59.

49 The *Online Etymology Dictionary* states that **Horace Walpole** coined the word in a January 28, 1754 letter to **Horace Mann** basing himself upon the name *Serendip*, a label for the island of Ceylon (modern Sri Lanka) derived from the Arabic *Sarandib* and the Sanskrit *Simhaladvipa* (or "Dwelling-Place-of-Lions Island"). Walpole instances a Persian fairy tale about three princes of Serendip who, as he puts it, "were always making discoveries, by accidents and sagacity, of things they were not in quest of." See http://www.etymonline.com/index.php?search=serendipity&searchmode=none.

50 Borges, "The Library of Babel" was originally published in the 1941 collection *El jardín de senderos que se bifurcan*, but was later integrated into *Ficciones* (1944). See *Collected Fictions*, trans. Andrew Hurley (New York: Viking, 1998).

51 **Angus Snead MacDonald**, "A Library of the Future," *Library Journal* 58 (Dec. 1 and 15, 1933): 974-5.

52 **Christopher D. Johnson**, *Myth, Metaphor, and Aby Warburg's Bildungatlas Mnemosyne* (Ithaca: Cornell University Press, 2012).

53 Johnson, *Myth, Metaphor, and Aby Warburg's Bildungatlas Mnemosyne*, emphasis ours.

54 **Henri Petroski** has dedicated a chapter to this topic in *The Book on the Book Shelf* (New York: Alfred A. Knopf, 1999), 192-214.

55 Naturally, there's a catch: though dark and cool, underground storage can be damp, particularly in a region with high water tables. So the construction process involved a massive trench built with slurry walls –slurry is a viscous liquid made from water mixed with bentonite; a rebar cage was then inserted and concrete was pumped in to form a shell. A secondary set of walls were also built to prevent leakage and rainwater intrusion. On this subject, see **Aaron Seward**, "In Detail> Joe and Rika Mansueto Library - Murphy/Jahn Designs Glass-Domed Library for the University of Chicago," *The Architect's Newspaper*, http://archpaper.com/news/articles.asp?id=5380, accessed August 10, 2013.

56 **Samuel Brown**, *Some Account of Itinerating Libraries and their Founder* (Edinburgh: W. Blackwood and Sons, 1856), 61.

57 These features are detailed in **William Brown**'s *Memoir Relative to Itinerating Libraries* (Edinburgh: A. Balfour and Co., n.d.), 5-16.

58 Cited from http://www.mealsgate.org.uk/perambulating-library.php.

59 **Melvil Dewey** with **Myrtilla Avery**, *Traveling Libraries – Field and Future of Traveling Libraries*, Bulletin 40, Home Education Department (Albany: University of the State of New

York, 1901), 3.

60 **Melvil Dewey** with **Myrtilla Avery**, *Traveling Libraries*, 7.

61 On the history of the Washington County Free Library, see http://www.whilbr.org/bookmobile/index.aspx. Titcomb herself reflected on her experiments, first with wagons and then with motorized vehicles in various reports, including **Mary Lemist Titcomb**, *A County Library: And On the Trail of the Book Wagon; Two Papers Read at the Meeting of the American Library Association* (June 1909).

62 The figures are derived from table 14 in *Public Library Statistics Bulletin* (1953: 9), **U.S. Department of Health, Education, and Welfare**; Office of Education.

63 Annual report, *Public Libraries in the United States*, **National Center for Education Statistics**, table 2. Cited at http://www.ala.org/research/librarystats/public/bookmobiles/bookmobilesu.

64 http://archive.org/texts/bookmobile.php#thebookmobile.

65 The protagonist of **Virginia Woolf**'s *Jacob's Room* experiences study under the Reading Room's dome as being inside "an enormous mind." *Jacob's Room* (Oxford: Oxford University Press, 2008), 147.

66 **Carole King**, "The Rise and Decline of Village Reading Rooms," *Rural History* (2009) 20.2: 163–186.

67 **Henry Solly**, *Working Men's Social Clubs and Educational Institutes*, revised by B. T. Hall (London: Simpkin, Marshall, Hamilton, Kent and Co., 1904), 41-2.

68 On this subject see **Christina Kiaer**, "Rodchenko in Paris," *October 75* (Winter 1996): 3-35 and **Leah Dickerman**, "The Propagandizing of Things," pp. 62-99 in Magdalena Dabrowski, Leah Dickerman, and Peter Galassi, **Aleksandr Rodchenko** (New York: Museum of Modern Art, 1998).

69 MacDonald, "A Library of the Future," 973, 1024.

70 For documentation of this project, led by the library's assistant director **Nate Hill**, see http://4thfloor.chattlibrary.org/. On the notion of maker spaces as a model for a user- rather than collections-centered rethinking of the library see, for instance, **Kristin Fontichiaro** in *Library 2020 – Today's Leading Visionaries Describe Tomorrow's Library*, ed. Joseph Janes (Lanham, Toronto, Plymouth: Scarecrow Press, 2013), 7-13.

71 Cited from http://www.cultura.rj.gov.br/apresentacao-espaco/biblioteca-parque-de-manguinhos; translation ours.

72 Cf. "We have aimed to develop our library as a working laboratory for all kinds of people rather than as a monumental reading palace for the comparatively few 'book worms.' By following that policy we have actually attained the ideal of making the library the 'People's University.'" MacDonald, "A Library of the Future," 1025. MacDonald also imagined his librarians as highly skilled teachers: "the equivalent of a staff of university professors, scientists and technical experts" (974).

73 For a number of views that converge with at least portions of this community-centric vision, see Section III (*Community*) and, in particular, **Susan Hildreth** in Janes, *Library 2020*, 71-103.

74 Much of this ongoing work is documented at http://www.librarytestkitchen.org/.

75 Correspondence of **F. Marion Crawford** to **Isabella Stewart Gardner**, August 23, 1896. With thanks to Kristin Parker, former archivist at the Gardner Museum.

76 **Guglielmo Marconi**, *Technical World Magazine* (October 1912): 145. There are numerous websites dedicated to collecting such false prognostications, among them one maintained by Wikiquote at http://en.wikiquote.org/wiki/Incorrect_predictions.

77 **E. L. Doctorow**, "A Generation Later," in William Gibson and Bruce Sterling, *The Difference Engine: 20th Anniversary Edition* (New York: Ballantine, 2011).

78 If **George Santayana** had been entirely correct about forgetting and the repetition of the past, then libraries would be great engines of futurology. That they aren't—that the accumulated records of our acts and things do not prevent us from reprising our errors—tells us something about the nature of history. The eternally-returning error, after all, not infrequently takes the outward form of the new, of change, even progress. And it's often by clinging too tightly to a sense of the past that the most destructive transformations are set in motion.

79 Many of the illustrated catalogs of the **Library Bureau** can now be consulted on Google Books, among them: *Illustrated Catalog of the Library Bureau – A Handbook of Library and Office Fittings and Supplies* (Boston: Library Bureau, 1890); *Classified Illustrated Catalog of the Library Bureau – A Handbook of Library and Office Fittings and Supplies* (Boston: Library Bureau, 1894); *Classified Illustrated Catalog of the Library Department of the Library Bureau – A Handbook of Library Fittings and Supplies* (Boston: Library Bureau, 1897); *Classified Illustrated Catalog of the Library Bureau – A Handbook of Library Fittings and Supplies* (Boston: Library Bureau, 1900); and *Library Catalog – A Descriptive List* (Boston: Library Bureau, 1904).

80 In similar fashion, **Andrew Carnegie**'s library program developed a basic pattern language for the public libraries it funded, but left most design decisions, from furnishings to the books in the collections, to locals. Contrast this with the recent conflict over the renovation of the New York Public Library's main branch on Fifth Avenue—a confection of consultants and starchitects, with little room for community input and fluid design thinking.

81 On pattern languages, once again, see Alexander, *A Pattern Language: Towns, Buildings, Construction*.

82 **John Ruskin**, *Stones of Venice*, in *The Works of John Ruskin* (New York: John B. Alden, 1885), 179.

83 For more on serendipity, see **Elinor Barber** and **Robert K. Merton**, *The Travels and Adventures of Serendipity: A Study in Sociological Semantics and the Sociology of Science* (Princeton: Princeton University Press, 2004).

84 **Rainer Maria Rilke**, "Primal Sound," in Jerome Rothenberg and Marta Ulvaeus, eds., *The Book of Music and Nature* (Middletown: Wesleyan University Press, 2001).

85 **Neil Gaiman**, interview at Bookpage.com, http://www.bookpage.com/the-book-case/2010/04/14/neil-gaiman-talks-about-his-love-of-libraries/, accessed July 22, 2013.

Cold Storage

> Because their memory is short-lived, humans accumulate an infinity of prostheses. Confronted with the teeming bazaars that result, panic sets in. They fear being trampled by a horde of writings, submerged beneath heaps of words. So, to ensure their freedom, they erect formidable fortresses.

With these words begins Alain Resnais's documentary film on the Bibliothèque Nationale de France, *Toute la mémoire du monde* (*All the World's Memory*; 1956). The camera rises up off the basement floor, emerging from amidst

the piles of books as if out of some primordial textual twilight. Here is a place at once carcereal and irenic, inside and outside of time: a depot where books arrive, await their destiny, are preserved for the world's memory or forgotten and reduced to dust. The camera is soon off to places less sepulchral. Its ultimate destination is the great hall where "torn from their world," books are fed to swarms of "paper crunching pseudo-insects": the loving, devouring species known as readers.

The present book ends where Resnais's documentary starts: stalking the floor of a formidable fortress, a high-density refrigerated vault known as the Harvard Depository (HD) wherein reside the 9.7 million books, pamphlets, posters, papers, films, magnetic tapes, photographs, and microforms that make up the bulk of university collections.

With its 200,000 square feet of storage space and three million linear feet of shelving, the HD represents the heart of Harvard's library system. It is, however, a dislocated heart, remote and prosthetic. Invisible to patrons, it is situated twenty five miles from campus atop a remote hill, within a guarded compound near Harvard's primate labs. From outside, it is a vast, faceless emplacement of corrugated concrete, situated on a grassy berm surrounded by a forest of frost-fringed maples interlaced with New England's mossy, tumbledown stone walls. Seven storage modules have been built to date; eight additional slots remain available to accommodate the continuation of the human record.

The HD is an analog server farm, comparable to and distinct from the actual server farms Harvard maintains in other off-site locations. It delivers physical packets of information via a pipeline of vans that shuttle back and forth to campus four times a day at approximately 60 miles per hour (or at about 0.00000009th the speed traveled by their digital brethren). Though built in 1968, its origins stretch back to the late nineteenth century when the then Harvard President, Charles William Eliot, was a pioneering advocate of off-site storage for little used collections.

As in patrician libraries of the early modern era, artifacts that reach the Depository are sorted by size once removed from the plastic bins in which they arrive. Each is baptized with a color dot, indicative of a volumetric rank. But here the avoidance of voids and pinpoint placement trump the patrician dream of a taxonomically or chromatically harmonious shelf.

The HD is a world designed for the eyes of laser scanners, inventory tracking systems, and mechanically-aided acts of retrieval. Its corridors are narrow and tall, devised to accommodate not inquisitive readers but the inhuman girth and reach of electrical lifts. The shelves are adjustable, calibrated to the varying dimensions of acid-neutral boxes contained in trays of exactly equal depth. Only the bottom fifth are visible to the pedestrian; laterally so, because the coded sidewalls of trays, not the spines of books, face outward. The HD reduces its sparsely-distributed human agents to parts in a cybernetic machine that speaks a language not of authors, subjects, and titles, but of barcode label identifiers and the ID numbers they encode. But even this networked state of the depository is a difference in degree and not kind, in vernacular rather than in tongue, from the state of the library in different times and places. Whether acting as mausoleum, database, or civic making space, libraries of different times and places can be understood as networks compounded of humans, systems, and material affordances, evolving to preserve and circulate things called books. HD's differences are of degree, albeit in extremis—to make the minimum viable use of humans as agents; to advance the interests of, and the prospects for, information systems and schema.

Like other time capsules of its kind, the Depository sets out to subjugate time as it compresses space. A robust and redundant cooling system maintains the main storage area at an average of 45 degrees Fahrenheit and at 35% average humidity. (Lop off five degrees and five percentage points in the case of the darkened den inhabited by film and video collections.)

The vault is sealed off on all sides with double doors granting access to the cargo bays plied by staff navigating whirring, wheeling shuttles, purpose-built to negotiate the vast stacks. Here the last vestiges of natural light yield to artificial illumination and electric eyes. Directed by database-generating charts, depository staff wield darting laser eyes that scan the shelves under the shy stare of ultraviolet-shielded fluorescent lights, capped with sensors to diminish long-term damage to media. They are cool to the touch and cold to the soul, even of gnats—although none have ever been sighted.

During the day, the HD has a monastic cast and a nocturnal feel. There's little talk and a great deal of sorting, sifting, stacking, and loading, both in forward and in reverse. Most of the stacks are cloaked in darkness. The few that are not whirr and squeal to the tune of forklifts performing the day's optimized paths of restitution and retrieval.

At night, the HD is freed from the distractions inflicted by the paper crunchers' proxies. As soon as they complete their appointed rounds, the decisive light switch is thrown, the last security code entered, and deadbolts bring the doors into lockstep with the walls. The hum of surveillance cameras and cooling fans recedes into the background. The vault is sealed tight.

An epiphany can be delayed no more.

Two competing tales are told about the event that is believed to transpire every evening at midnight (even if unheard by mortal ears and unseen by mortal eyes).

According to some, music erupts: the celestial song of millions of works, recorded in every medium, in every language, in every country that has ever existed, is sung. According to others, a deafening silence reigns in the midst of a no less sublime spectacle of universal immobility. Books rub up against other books, typefaces touch in secret, imperceptible conversations are carried on across the shelves and across the centuries that deride the petty illusions of the living; molecular mutations gnaw away at monuments of celluloid and cellulose that have successfully stood every test that time has thrust their way; dust motes dance and dart.

Our collective ark filled with petabyte upon petabyte of memories sets sail on the sea of history: humankind's noblest endeavor (oblivion is the destination).

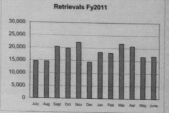

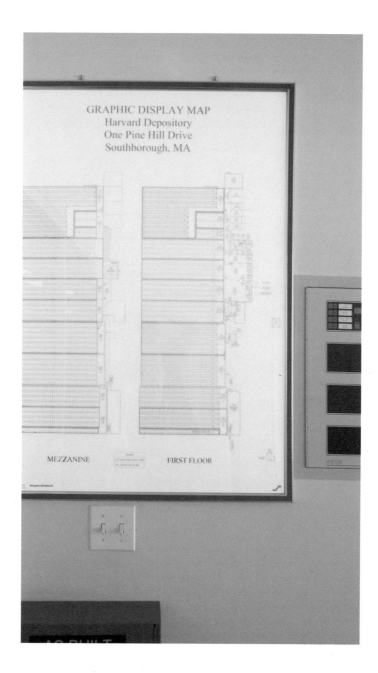

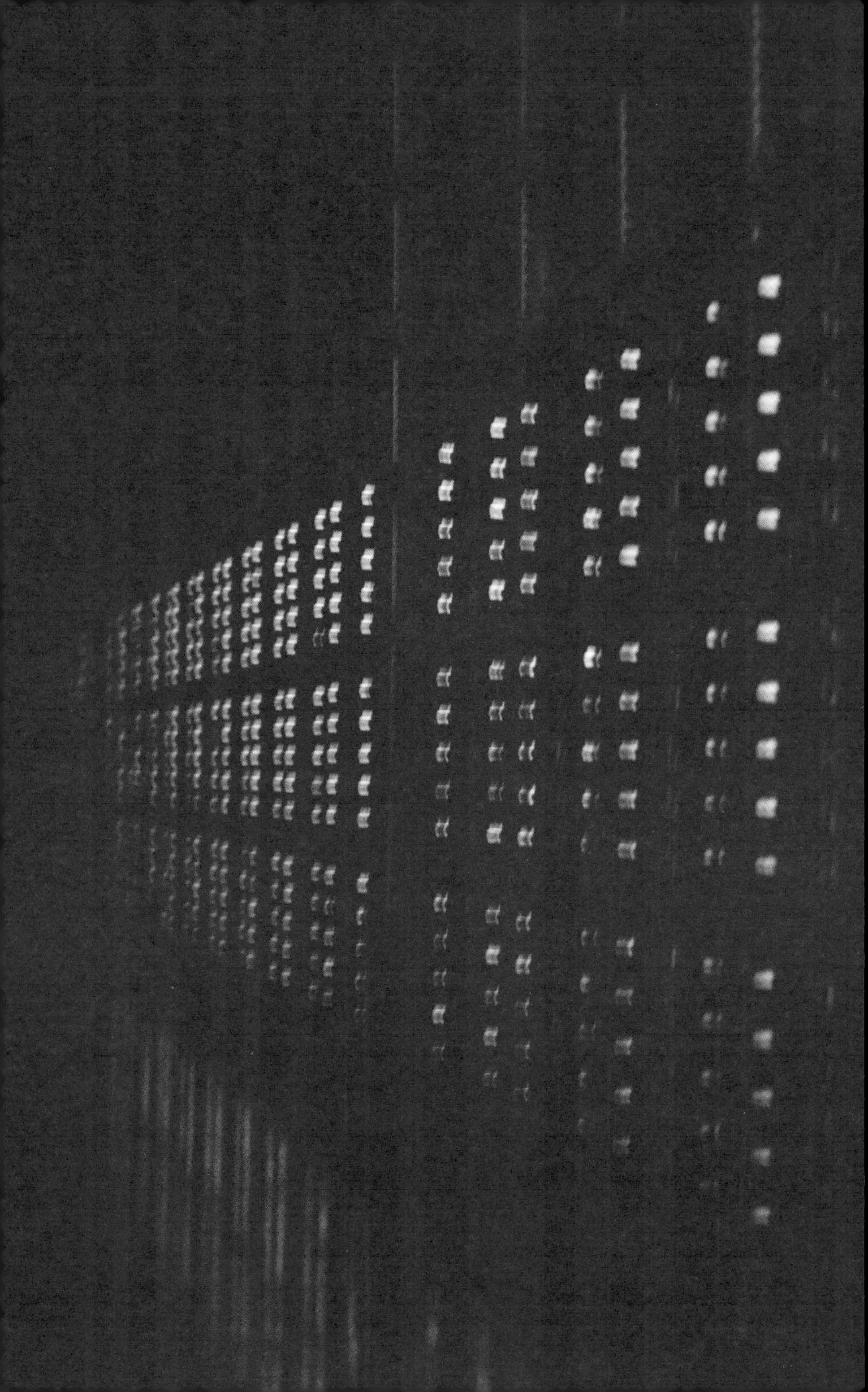

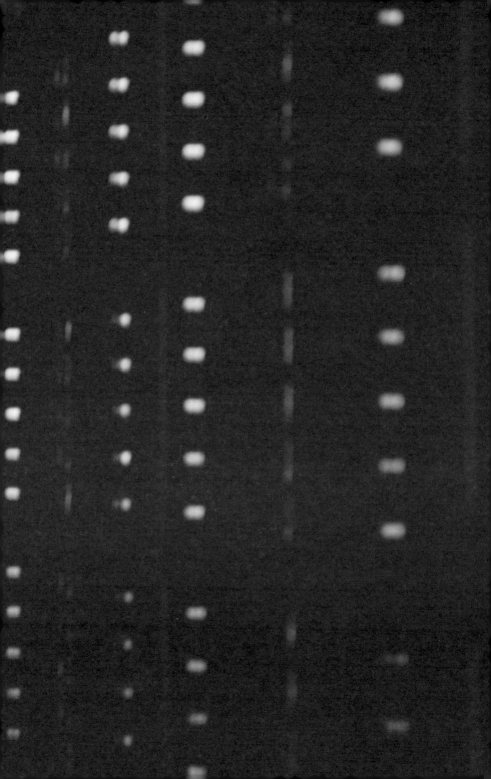

Linkography

http://4thfloor.chattlibrary.org
http://ala.org
http://archive.org/about/#future
http://bexarbibliotech.org
http://bibliophemera.blogspot.com
http://bl.uk
http://bnf.fr/fr/acc/x.accueil.html
http://bpl.org
http://cultura.rj.gov.br/espaco/biblioteca-parque-de-manguinhos
http://dnb.de
http://digital-librarian.com
http://dp.la
http://europeana.eu
http://folger.edu
http://futuristspeaker.com/2006/11/the-future-of-libraries
http://getty.edu/research
http://ideastore.co.uk
http://ifla.org
http://ilibrariana.wordpress.com
http://ipl.org
http://knightfoundation.org/future-libraries
http://kulturhuset.stockholm.se/TioTretton
http://lib.harvard.edu
http://lib.ncsu.edu/huntlibrary/vision
http://libraryasincubatorproject.org
http://librarylab.law.harvard.edu
http://librarytestkitchen.org
http://loc.gov/index.html
http://longnow.org
http://mansueto.lib.uchicago.edu
http://marybakereddylibrary.org/collections/research/ask-a-researcher/reading-rooms
http://museumplantinmoretus.be
http://ndl.go.jp/en
http://newberry.org
http://nypl.org/collections/labs
http://projectinfolit.org
http://spl.org
http://trove.nla.gov.au/general/api
http://warburg.sas.ac.uk/library/maps

Acknowledgments

As alluded to toward the end of our essay, *The Library Beyond the Book* was born not as a book project but as a series of design studios held at Harvard's Graduate School of Design. These began in the fall 2011 semester as *Bibliotheca: The Library Past/Present/Future* and continued from the spring 2012 semester to the present as *Library Test Kitchen* (http://www.librarytestkitchen.org/).

The studios in question arose in the context of two conversations located at the crossroads between the analog and the digital worlds. One concerned the reorganization of the Harvard library system; the other, the design of the Digital Public Library of America—two separate conversations but with a shared agenda in the shape of some fundamental questions:

What form could or should the library of the twenty-first century assume? Should it simply vanish into virtual desktops and merge into a timeless and placeless universal database? Should it adopt a double identity, bridging the worlds of print and digital documents, of physical presence and telepresence? Should it alter its identity and become a workshop, a laboratory, an innovation incubator where emerging and future forms interact and dialogue with the relics of the past? Or should it simply merge with the university itself as a place of knowledge production and reproduction? If so, where then should books "go" in the twenty-first century? And how about all the other "old media" that make up the record of human civilizations?

Big questions all—the quotation is from the fall 2011 *Bibliotheca* syllabus—but the focus of the studios was as much on big visions as on small answers: critically and historically informed solutions to real-world problems based on field research and applied design thinking. The motto was "building the library of the future one component at a time." The family of components soon grew to encompass new rule sets for reading spaces, designs for carrels as collaboration spaces, reading booths that serve as "cold spots," scanning stations that expose the social history of the books being scanned, books that ping readers on the basis of their prior search histories, reference desks that serve as knowledge exhibition and performance spaces, and real-time live and emerging event bulletin boards.

However much the work of its two authors, *The Library Beyond the Book* bears traces of this collective endeavor on every page. The provocations that flicker along the book's margins were inspired by the ideas of numerous studio participants, foremost among them Joshua Kaufman, an early member of the authorial team in the book's brainstorming phases and the author also of the splendid photographs featured in the concluding photo-essay. No less radiantly present in the book's argument are John Palfrey (who co-taught the original *Bibliotheca* seminar in 2011), Jeff Goldenson (who has co-led *Library Test Kitchen* from 2012 to the present), Ann Whiteside (director of the Loeb Design Library and a key participant in the studios from the outset), Ben Brady (who participated in *Bibliotheca* as a student and then served as a teaching fellow in 2012), and Jessica Yurkofsky (who participated in and co-taught *Library Test Kitchen* along with Ben). We are grateful to all of them as well as to the many colleagues who contributed their time and energies to *Bibliotheca* and *Library Test Kitchen* in one form or another: among them Mohsen Mostafavi, Ann Blair, Leah Price, Robert Darnton, Sue Kriegsman, Mary Lee Kennedy, Mary Clare Althofen, Gregory Nagy, and Alex Csiszar.

Three other institutions also made key contributions to the present endeavor. The first is the leadership and community of the Berkman Center for Internet and Society where remarkable colleagues such as John Palfrey, David Weinberger, Peter Suber, and Stuart Shieber, among many others, have routinely enriched our thinking regarding libraries real or potential. The second is the Harvard Library Lab, without whose support neither *Bibliotheca* nor *Library Test Kitchen* would have been possible. The third is the Harvard Depository whose management and staff facilitated both repeated field trips related to the design studios and the *Cold Storage* photo shoot. We are eager to acknowledge the significance of all of their support.

The art director for the metaLABprojects series, Daniele Ledda, has pored with characteristic brilliance and tenacity over every detail of this, the inaugural volume in the series and we thank him for his fundamental work, as we do key collaborators at Harvard University Press, in particular Michael Fisher, without whose energy and enthusiasm the metaLABprojects series couldn't have come about.

We reserve a final, special thank you for Joe Alterio, whose nimble ink imaginings so playfully animate Melvil Dewey's time travels in this book's opening pages. We scripted the cartoon, but it was Joe who brought it to life.

Credits

Valuable image research assistance for this project was provided by Caitlin Christian-Lamb. The photographs featured in *Cold Storage* were taken by Joshua Kaufman on April 2, 2012 at the Harvard Depository in Southboro, Massachusetts for purposes of this book.

Author Key to *Provocations*

The brief thought experiments that figure in the book's margins were mostly generated within the setting of *Bibliotheca* and *Library Test Kitchen*; subsequently, they were revised and rewritten by the present book's main authors. The original source of each is indicated by means of the following initials; most have multiple authors.

AC - Annie Cain
AW - Ann Whiteside
BB - Ben Brady
GP - Gabrielle Patawaran
JG - Jeff Goldenson
JK - Joshua Kaufman
JP - John Palfrey
JS - Jeffrey T. Schnapp
JY - Jessica Yurkofsky
MB - Matthew Battles
MP – Matthew Phillips
NR - Nicolas Rivard
SM - Stacy Morton